Dry
Bones
Can Live
Again

The hand of the Lord was upon me, and carried me out in the spirit of the Lord, and set me down in the midst of the valley which was full of bones,

And caused me to pass by them round about: and, behold, there were many in the open valley; and, lo, they were very dry.

And He said unto me, Son of man, can these bones live? And I answered, O Lord God, thou knowest.

Again He said unto me, Prophesy upon these bones, and say unto them, O ye dry bones, hear the word of the Lord.

Thus saith the Lord God unto these bones; Behold, I will cause breath to enter into you, and ye shall live:

And I will lay sinews upon you, and will bring up flesh upon you, and cover you with skin, and put breath in you, and ye shall live; and ye shall know that I am the Lord.

Ezekiel 37:1–6

DRY
BONES
CAN LIVE
AGAIN

Revival in the Local Church

Robert E. Coleman

Fleming H. Revell Company
Old Tappan, New Jersey

ACKNOWLEDGMENT

Grateful acknowledgment is made to the many authors and publishers whose works are cited in this book. Every effort has been made to give proper credit for all quoted material. Where copyright laws apply, permission to use the quotation has been granted, and when requested by the publisher this permission is indicated in the footnote.

Seventh Printing

Contents

Introduction

A DEEPENING CRISIS

Men everywhere are sensing that something is missing in the life of the church. We have a form of religion but no power. For most churchmen, there is no thrill in personal devotions; no spring in the step; no shout in the soul. The joy of sacrifice is gone. Complacency is the norm.

While the church flounders in mediocrity, the world plunges deeper into sin. For the average person life has lost its meaning. It is eat, drink and be merry, with every man for himself. The sacredness of home and family is forsaken. Standards of decency in public and private are debased. A spirit of lawlessness pervades the land.

But the day of reckoning is sure to come. Moral and spiritual decline has its limits. There comes a time when we must reap the folly of our ways. Already we are beginning to see the disintegration of enduring values in society, and unless something happens soon to change our course, civilization as we know it is on its way out.

NEED OF THE HOUR

Yet there is hope. Dry bones can live again. In other days of crises when catastrophe has threatened, men have turned unto the Lord and found in him deliverance and strength. In fact, our greatest spiritual awakenings have come during the darkest periods of church history. Perhaps again the peril of the age may bring us to our senses.

Even now there are some encouraging signs. The growing lay witness movement, the multiplication of Bible study and prayer groups, the emergence of leadership in student evangelism, the response to great evangelistic crusades, the new concern for Christian mission in the church—these, and many other currents of contemporary religious life, evidence an awakening concern.

Despite the superficiality of much that goes on in the church, increasing numbers of people are seeking something real. They may not be theologians, but they have enough sense to know that God is alive, and they long to know Him in personal experience. Ceremonial rites and pious clichés, however orthodox, do not satisfy the heart. Nor does all the glitter of big programs, big budgets, big buildings and big mergers answer the cry of the soul for spiritual reality.

Call it what you may, these people are searching for revival—a God-wrought transformation in the inner man that reaches into the total fabric of our life and culture. Here is the challenge of our day, and unless we face it courageously, we are not being relevant to the situation.

WHY THIS MANUAL

This book is designed to help you examine the issue. It seeks to bring revival into focus—what it is, how it comes, when it may be expected—and to propose a practical way through which you can work for revival in your church.

The emphasis of the book is upon principles of revival—considerations that are basic to any deeper life ministry. It may be used as a general study on revival or, in a more specific sense, it may be used as a preparation manual for special revival services in the church. But in any case, it is intended as a source book for personal and group study.

In recognition of the busy churchman, only the most vital matters are presented, and the treatment is very brief. However, an attempt is made to encourage further research by documenting resources and noting some helpful bibliographic references.

The value of the book lies in the extent to which you permit yourself to become involved with the subject. Try to complete the assignments. Make personal applications. And as you do, earnestly pray: "Lord, send a revival, and let it begin with me!"

1 - The Blessing of Revival

The Psalmist prayed: "Wilt thou not revive us again: that thy people may rejoice in thee?" (Psalm 85:6). He recognized that the people of God were spiritually impotent, the fires of devotion were burning low, their joy was gone. "Revive us," he cried, but what did he mean by it? What is "revival?"

Most people today think of "revival" as a series of protracted meetings designed to whip up interest in the Church. Others tend to look upon it as some kind of excited emotionalism in religion. Yet I doubt if these popular associations of the term ever entered the mind of the person who offered this prayer.

COMING ALIVE

"Revival" means to wake up and live. In the Old Testament, the word comes from a root meaning "to live," which originally conveyed the idea of "breathing," inasmuch as breath is the expression of life in all animate beings. Hence, it could be said of the dry bones: ". . . I will cause breath to enter into you, and ye shall live" (Ezekiel 37:5; compare 37:6, 14; Job 33:4; I Kings 17:22). Revival, or life, was "breathing in the breath of God." As used here in the causa-

11

tive sense—the form more often translated "revival"—the word underscores the source of this life in God.[1]

In the New Testament the comparable word means "to live again" (Revelation 20:5; Romans 14:9; compare 7:9). As Jesus used the term, it denotes the change in the life of a penitent prodigal who returned to the Father's house, in the sense that the Son who was "dead" is now "alive again" (Luke 15:24, 32). Other words liken revival to the rekindling of a slowly dying fire (II Timothy 1:6) or to a plant which has put forth fresh shoots and "flourished again" (Philippians 4:10).[2]

The basic idea always is the return of something to its true nature and purpose. When this concept is applied to redemptive history, revival can be seen as that "strange and sovereign work of God in which He visits His own people, restoring, reanimating and releasing them into the fullness of His blessing." [3] By its power "vast energies, hitherto slumbering, are awakened, and new forces—for long preparing under the surface—burst into being." [4] Life is in its wake—

---

[1] Altogether this word is used in its various forms more than 250 times in the Old Testament, of which about 55 are in the Piel or causative construction in Hebrew. Some examples may be found in Genesis 7:3; 19:32, 34; Deuteronomy 6:24; 32:39; I Kings 20:31; II Kings 7:4; Nehemiah 4:2; Job 36:6; Psalms 41:2; 71:20; 80:18; 119:25, 37, 40, 50, 88, 93, 107, 147, 154, 156, 159; 138:7; 143:11; Jeremiah 49:11; Ezekiel 13:18; Hosea 6:3; 14:7; Habakkuk 3:2, to cite a few. It may be translated as *revive, live, restore, preserve, heal, prosper, flourish, save* or some other similar term.

[2] A word for revival is used only seven times in the Greek New Testament, although the idea is suggested in other ways. Perhaps one reason for the sparing use of this term, as compared to the Old Testament, is because the New Testament narrative covers only a generation, during which time the Church, for the most part, enjoyed a remarkable degree of spiritual life.

[3] Stephen F. Olford, *Heart Cry for Revival* (Westwood, N. J.: Fleming H. Revell, 1962), p. 17. This little book of expository sermons on revival is solidly Biblical and warmly written. It is excellent reading on this subject. A comparable book is A. Skevington Wood's, *And with Fire* (Fort Washington, Pa.: Christian Literature Crusade, 1958).

[4] James Burns, *Revivals, Their Laws and Leaders* (Grand Rapids: Baker, 1960), p. 39. First published in 1909, this book is a classic in its

life at its best, life in its fullness, life overflowing with the love and power of God.

Not everything about this new life can be fully explained, of course. Being a supernatural work of the Spirit, there is always the element of mystery about it.[5] But one thing is clear—in revival men come alive to the life of God.

PERSONAL TRANSFORMATION

Evidence of revival is the change wrought in the hearts of men by the Holy Spirit. The extent of its penetration will vary, and there will be differences in the mode of its expression, but something of its presence is manifest "wherever you see (spiritual life) rising from a state of comparative depression to a tone of increased vigor and strength."[6]

The most immediate transformation is in the renewal of individual Christian experience. When one responds fully to Divine grace, there is a wonderful assurance of sins forgiven; the heart is clean; the soul is free. Faith does not stagger at the promises of God. Prayer pulsates with the fragrance of heaven. Love fills the heart with singing and there is spontaneous praise of the Most High. There is still suffering and temptation, but amid it all is the light of God's face shining in the inner man. Christ is real; His peace sweeps over the soul; His victory overcomes the world.

When viewed from the standpoint of New Testament Christianity, actually there is nothing unusual about this experience. It is the way that a person should always live.

---

field. Its treatment of laws observable in revivals is unsurpassed for beauty and simplicity of expression. Andrew W. Blackwood has written two summary chapters in this reprint edition.

[5] In *Revival, An Enquiry* (London: SMC Press, 1954), p. 14, Max Warren correctly observes that true revival is continuous and changing, and therefore "any finality of assessment would be premature." With a development so "alive" as this, the "attempt to pigeon-hole it is futile, for the pigeon will not stay in the hole."

[6] William B. Sprague, *Lectures on Revival of Religion* (London: The Banner of Trust, 1959), pp. 7, 8.

Revival simply brings out what it is to be normal. To use the words of Roy Hession, it is "just you and I walking along the highway in complete oneness with the Lord Jesus and with one another, with cups continually cleansed and overflowing with the life and love of God." [7] Or interpreting it like Charles G. Finney, revival simply "consists in obeying God," [8] which means that it is the most elemental duty of man.

In this personal sense, revival should be a constant reality. The idea that it is "a thing of special times and seasons" [9] owes its inception to the inconsistent nature of man and not to the will of God. Unfortunately, for most of us, despite our professions there comes those periods of spiritual sluggishness which make revival necessary. But if we lived in the continual fullness of the Spirit of Christ, as God desires, revival would be an abiding state of experience.[10]

---

[7] Roy Hession, *The Calvary Road* (London: Christian Literature Crusade, n.d.), p. 31.

[8] Charles G. Finney, *Revivals of Religion* (Westwood, New Jersey: Fleming H. Revell, n.d.), p. 1. This volume consisting of twenty-two lectures has remained in print for more than a hundred years and is probably the most influential text on the subject.

[9] Arthur Wallis, *In the Day Of Thy Power* (London: Christian Literature Crusade), p. 19. The author in this excellent book prefers to think of revival in terms of great mass movements which stand out in history. As to what usually is given recognition, his point may be well taken, but I see no need to limit revival to these spectacular and occasional displays of God's sovereign power.

[10] An excellent treatment of this idea is Norman P. Grubb's little book, *Continuous Revival* (Fort Washington, Pa.: Christian Literature Crusade). The author mentions how he was shaken out "of the misconception of years, that revival could only come in great soul-shaking outpourings of the Spirit." Of course, he rejoices in the times when the church was mightily stirred in "precious hurricanes of the Spirit," but as he says, "I saw the defeatism and almost hopelessness that so many of us had fallen into by thinking that we could do nothing except pray, often rather unbelievingly, and wait until the heavens rent and God came down. But now I see 'revival' in its truest sense is an everyday affair right down within the reach of everyday folk to be experienced in our hearts, homes and churches, and in our fields of service. When it does break forth in greater and more public ways, thank God; but meanwhile we can see to it that we are being ourselves constantly revived persons, which of course also means that others are getting revived in our own circles." (*Ibid.*, p. 6.)

OUTGOING LOVE

Yet revival involves more than personal blessing. Invariably as individuals come alive to the reality of Christ, and this experience is multiplied in the lives of others, the church feels a new unity of faith and purpose—a genuine fellowship in the Spirit.[11] Times of revival are times when God's people come together and minor differences are resolved in the larger commitment to their common mission.[12]

The love of Christ filling our hearts moves us to care for those whom God loves and for whom He gave His Son. Out of this holy compassion the dynamic for a compelling evangelism and social concern is born. Duty becomes a joy. In revival we want to help the oppressed and afflicted.[13] Love naturally overflows when hearts are full.

---

[11] Max Warren distinguishes between "revival" as a church directed movement and "enthusiasm" as more of an individualistic expression of experience. He observes that personal enthusiasm outside the structure of the Church usually results in magnifying personal blessings to the detriment of the larger body of believers, and often ends in schism. Very likely this observation oversimplifies the situation, but it at least points up a real danger in revival movements. (*Op. cit.*, pp. 19–37.)

[12] Genuine revival is the key to any ecumenical movement since it brings out the dynamics of true Christian unity. This has been demonstrated in the history of the Church. If popular spokesmen of the drive for church union were as much concerned for spiritual revival as organizational structure I believe that there would be more progress in true Christian unity.

[13] Revival is a catalyst of social reformation. It produces the kind of concern and environment for things to happen that can radically change human behavior and institutions. Merely to try to improve human conditions by social action alone does not solve the basic problem in society. This is the fallacy of the so-called modern "social gospel," which does not come to grips with the basic problem of sin in the human heart. Until something is done to regenerate the sinful nature of man, any social program is superficial. On the other hand, the life changing gospel of Christ has a clear social application, and until this is realized in practical situations, we have not understood its relevance to our whole life. Genuine revival fuses together in love the personal and social aspects of the gospel. Again, a study of church history will bear out this conclusion. Contrary to the impression given by many liberal theologians, the great humanitarian movements of civilization have had their roots deep in evangelical revivals of religion. For example, in recent centuries influences that grew out of revivals gave birth to the movement for the abolition of slavery, the organization of trade unions, abolition of child

Inevitably society feels the impact. As the Gospel goes forth in word and deed, the world takes note that men have been with Jesus. Conviction of sin settles down. Sinners are moved to seek the Saviour. Restitutions are made. Broken homes are reunited. Moral standards in the community are lifted. Integrity makes its way into the government. To the extent that the Spirit of revival prevails, mercy, justice and righteousness sweep over the land.

HUMAN SHORTCOMINGS

In all fairness, however, we should recognize that there are human circumstances in any situation which restrain the outreach of revival. Materialism, for example, is a deterrent to its spread. Or it might be a cultural prejudice that refuses to yield to the new spirit of love. For that matter, any perversion of righteousness will hinder revival, whether it is conscious or not. Since society is infiltrated completely by man's depravity, revival will always have an uphill battle.

The opposition will be most pronounced from those who do not want a spiritual dimension of life. Some will be re-

---

labor, women's suffrage, hundreds of benevolent and missionary societies, the founding of our first colleges, the Sunday-school movement, Bible societies, the YMCA, just to mention a few. The modern social gospel itself actually grew out of the mid-nineteenth century revivals, although in time the humanitarian concern has tended to lose much of its evangelical content. A well-documented study of this thesis, a Ph.D. dissertation at Harvard, is Timothy Smith's *Revivalism and Social Reform* (New York: Abingdon Press, 1957). J. Edwin Orr's Ph.D. dissertation at Oxford, published as *The Second Evangelical Awakening in Britain* (London: Marshall, Morgan and Scott, 1949), also brings out the tremendous social effect of these nineteenth-century revivals, as does his more recent study, *The Light of the Nations* (Grand Rapids: Wm. B. Eerdmans, 1965). A less extensive approach to the subject is Frank G. Beardsley's *Religious Progress Through Religious Revival* (New York: American Tract Society, 1943). What is carefully documented by these scholars in reference to this period of history is but an illustration of a principle that applies at any time a dynamic evangelism prevails upon men. A broad review of the state of social concern today among evangelicals may be found in Sherwood Wert's book, *The Social Conscience of the Evangelical* (New York: Harper & Row, 1968).

pelled by the personal ethic of the revival; others will resent its social implications. Anytime practical holiness is manifest, antagonism can be expected from the carnal mind that is enmity against God.

We should remember, too, that there are still obvious human limitations among those who are revived. Regrettable as it may seem, spiritual renewal does not make one any less a man. Ignorance, emotional instability, personality quirks, and all the other traits of our fallen humanity, are very much in evidence. Though the revival is not responsible for these shortcomings, it has to bear their reproach.[14]

THE DIVINE HALLMARK

Nevertheless, wherever the spirit of revival is felt, attention focuses not upon human weakness but upon divine power. It reveals One who makes the earth His footstool and who sees nations of men as dust on the scales of His judgment. In the might of His holy arm, "human personalities are overshadowed, and human programs abandoned." Man retires "into the background because God has taken the field." [15] In stripping away the artificiality of human achievements revival creates a situation where the grace of God is magnified. Christ is lifted up and men bow in adoration before Him.

Overshadowing it all is the awe inspiring reality of "the presence of the Lord" (Acts 3:19). This is the witness of revival which has no counterfeit—the overwhelming sense of the Holy Spirit drawing men to Christ and making them an instrument of blessing to others. Where this is in evidence, the world has to admit that God is alive.

---

[14] Because revival does release the soul from bondage, it is not surprising that excessive demonstrations of spiritual freedom sometimes occur. In this sense, as Max Warren observes, "revival is a perilous experience." But, he wisely concludes, "the perils must be set beside the perils of Laodicea. More often than not there is the choice." Max Warren, *op. cit.*, p. 21.

[15] Arthur Wallis, *op. cit.*, p. 20.

SOME ACCOUNTS OF REVIVAL

Take a few examples. Jonathan Edwards, renowned pastor at Northampton, Massachusetts, might be cited as one witness. Describing the effect of a great outpouring of the Spirit in his parish in 1735, he says:

As the number of true saints multiplied . . . the town seemed to be full of the presence of God: it never was so full of love, nor of joy, and yet so full of distress, as it was then. There were remarkable tokens of God's presence in almost every house. It was a time of joy in families on account of salvation being brought unto them. . . . On whatever occasions persons met together, Christ was to be heard of and seen in the midst of them. . . . The Spirit of God began to be so wonderfully poured out in a general way through the town, people had soon done with their old quarrels, backbitings, and intermeddling with other men's matters. The tavern was soon left empty. Every day seemed in many respects like a Sabbath day.[16]

Edwards noted, too, that "there were many instances of persons who came from abroad on visits" to the town, who "partook of that shower of divine blessing," and, as these visitors "went home rejoicing," soon "the same work began to prevail in several other towns in the country." [17]

The Korean revival early in this century is another example of what happens when the Spirit of God takes over. A missionary who was present at a church meeting during the flood tide of this outpouring says:

---

[16] Jonathan Edwards, *A Faithful Narrative of the Surprising Word of God in the Conversion of Many Hundred Souls in Northampton and the Neighboring Towns and Villages,* in *Puritan Sage, Collected Writings of Jonathan Edwards,* ed. by Vergilus Ferm (New York: Library Publishers, 1958), pp. 169, 170, 177.

[17] *Ibid.,* p. 171.

The room was full of God's presence . . . a feeling
of God's nearness impossible to describe. . . . The whole
audience began to pray. . . . It was not many, but one,
born of one Spirit, lifted to one Father above. . . . God
came to us in Pyeng Yang that night. . . . Man after
man would arise, confess his sin, break down and weep.
. . . My last glimpse of the audience is photographed
indelibly in my brain. Some threw themselves full length
on the floor, hundreds stood with arms out-stretched
towards heaven. Every man forgot each other. Each was
face to face with God.[18]

As is true in every genuine revival, the overflow of God's
Spirit did not cease with the blessing of the people gathered
for prayer at Pyeng Yang. The account goes on to say that
when the men returned to their homes in the country, they
took the Pentecostal fire with them.

Everywhere the story was told the same Spirit flowed
forth and spread. Practically every church . . . throughout the peninsula received its share of blessings. . . .
All through the city men were going from house to house,
confessing to individuals they had injured, returning
stolen property and money, not only to Christians, but to
non-Christians as well. The whole city was stirred.[19]

In a more recent setting, the events leading to the consecration of the new cathedral in Coventry, England, in 1962,
furnish an example of a contemporary renewal experience.
Stephen Verney, an Anglican priest, tells how a group of
laity and clergy got together to seek the Lord. As they al-

---

[18] Told by Dr. William N. Blair in his book *Gold in Korea,* and quoted
by Kyang Chek Hon in his address included in *One Race, One Gospel,
One Task,* Vol. I (Minneapolis: World Wide Publications, 1967), pp.
109–111. Used by permission.
[19] *Ibid.,* p. 112.

lowed love, humility and prayer to flow through them, "a deep sense of the presence of God" filled their lives.

Out of this fellowship the idea formed for a deeper life mission which eventually involved the whole diocese. In describing the wonderful result, Verney says:

> The more deeply people were involved, the more clearly was God calling them to go deeper still, and to offer Him the obedience of their whole lives. . . . The diocese became a person, a body alive with a spirit. . . . We became a loving family with a purpose. . . . We experienced an extraordinary outburst of worship and happiness. . . . Great services were held in the new cathedral, offering up to God every part of our daily lives. . . . We have seen reality break through, like the sun through a fog, sweeping away the pretenses. People have been set free, to become what they really are. We have begun to know that a whole diocese could be a fellowship of the Holy Spirit.[20]

There it is again. That same sense of the divine Presence thrilling the Church with reality of life and mission.

A PERSONAL WITNESS

To these accounts I might add one of the most vivid experiences of revival in my own life. It climaxed in February of 1950 on the campus of Asbury College in Kentucky. For a time the Spirit manifested Himself in such power that classes had to be suspended, and day and night for nearly a week we simply waited upon God. Before the initial effect of the revival had subsided, practically every person on the campus knew what it was to feel the touch of heaven. As

---

[20] Stephen Verney, *Fire in Conventry* (Westwood: Fleming H. Revell, 1964), pp. 24, 26, 35, 36, 51.

the witness was carried by Spirit-filled students and faculty to neighboring cities and states, thousands more were converted or awakened in a new way to Christian obedience. The emotional intensity of those thrilling days passed, but the reality of God which we experienced still continues in the lives of many.

During the first days of the revival the little college community became "an island of prayer" attracting persons for miles around by its other-worldly atmosphere.[21] Reporters who came to see what was happening were awestruck by the magnetism of the movement. One reported, "I have never seen such happy people." Hearing the prayers, confessions, testimonies, and singing in a setting of such transparent sincerity, he called it an "unbelievable demonstration of religion." [22] Some cameramen with NBC Television had tears in their eyes as they reverently moved about taking films of the proceedings. The men representing the press seemed to be aware that they were walking on holy ground. One reporter, unaccustomed to such things, "stated that it seemed an intrusion to be present." [23]

Indeed, it was like being transported to another world—a world in which our spirits were truly free. For the most part we were utterly honest with ourselves and with one another.

---

[21] "College Revival Turns Marathon," Associated Press, *Dallas Morning News*, February 25, 1950. Almost every newspaper in America carried stories of this revival from February 23 to March 1. Some of the Kentucky newspapers during this period devoted several columns to it along with photographs.

[22] Edwin Leavers, "Impressions of Asbury Revival as Witnessed by Editor," *The Community News,* I, 44, Lexington, Ky., March 3, 1950, quoted in Henry C. James, *Halls Aflame* (Wilmore, Ky.: Department of Evangelism, Asbury Theological Seminary, 1966), pp. 47, 48. This book, written by one converted in the 1950 Asbury Revival, is a graphic account of the events which transpired during those days. It is interesting that at about this time similar revivals broke out on other college campuses across America, such as Wheaton and Houghton. See Fred W. Hoffman, *Revival Times in America* (Boston: W. A. Wilde, 1956), pp. 164–168.

[23] W. Curry Mavis, "Revival Tides Are Rising," *The Christian Minister,* II, 1, April, 1950, p. 1.

The sham of superficial religion was gone. Praise of God was as natural as breathing. All we wanted was for Christ to be exalted and His will done on earth as it is in heaven. A convert of the revival expressed it when he wrote home to his parents:

How I wish you were here. It is wonderful what the Lord is doing. I have such peace and joy I can't express it. I can't write much because I have been in heaven for three days, eaten three meals, had about three blessings, and walked about three hundred miles telling people that Jesus saves. . . . People are coming from all over trying to figure it out.[24]

One of the thousands who came was a prominent basketball coach in the state. He has written his first impression:

My most vivid memory of that day was when I opened the door of Hughes Auditorium. Although I could not explain it then, I know now that it was the Presence of the Holy Spirit. There was a certain feeling about His Presence that gave me a sense of peace and surrender. . . . Several students were kneeling at the altar, and a young man was on the platform exhorting. Afterward a series of young people came to the platform and gave their testimonies. Many told of the calls they had received during the meeting to go to foreign mission fields. Many said they had found the Lord for the first time, while others spoke of spiritual victories in their homes where mothers, fathers, brothers, and sisters had been converted during the last forty-eight hours. One could tell those testimonies were real and convincing. I was so impressed and so moved by the Holy Spirit

---

[24] Herbert Van Vorce, in a personal letter quoted by Henry C. James, *op. cit.*, p. 36.

that I could not fight any longer the call of God for my life. I made my way to the altar and very quietly but sincerely surrendered my life to Him.[25]

WONDERFUL VARIETY

What this young man experienced could be duplicated in some way every time there is revival. Yet, as we have seen, the particular manner in which revival comes will be different in each case. The spirit of the time, local circumstances, personal leadership, temperament of the people, and many other natural conditions, combine to give each revival its own peculiar color. This explains, in part, why methods employed in revival may vary in different times and among different people.[26]

While basic spiritual principles are common to all, so different is the way these principles emerge in a human situation that it is impossible to predict their precise form. God seems to delight in surprising His people with the unexpected freshness of His approach.

We can be grateful for this variety in God's providence, for it demonstrates that He is ever seeking to make His will more intelligible to His people. Yet it also serves to remind us that God is able, when He pleases, to confound the schemes of men. The spirit of the Lord is never put in a straitjacket of human manipulation. What He does in revival is by His own sovereign power, and no man dare take any credit for the work.

---

[25] Jimmy Rose, quoted in *ibid.*, p. 20. This young coach later became a Methodist minister and is now serving the church as a conference evangelist.

[26] A running summary of the way methods are adapted to changing cultures and conditions may be found in the recent book by Panlus Scharpff, *History of Evangelism* (Grand Rapids: Wm. B. Eerdmans, 1966). This study of the historical and theological roots of modern evangelism traces the forward thrust of the gospel in Germany, England and America for the past three hundred years.

THE WAY OF PROGRESS

However, irrespective of the way they may appear, revivals are the high peaks in religious experience. Whether in individual experience or the corporate life of the Church, it is during these times of refreshing when the work of the Holy Spirit is brought into bold relief.[27] Redemptive history could actually be written from the standpoint of these recurring revivals. Of course, in the sense that revival represents vital Christianity, it can be said, in varying degrees, that a deep revival undercurrent is always present in the spiritual life of the Church. But there are seasons when this stream breaks forth in great power affecting many people and sometimes changing the course of nations.

This can be seen frequently in the Old Testament, but it comes to its fruition at Pentecost with the emergence of the New Testament church. For three centuries the Spirit of revival, continued to dominate the persecuted and impoverished Christian community. However, as the church gained in worldly prestige, eventually being recognized as the state religion of Rome in the fourth century, spiritual fervor noticeably declined.

Though somewhat smothered by the ecclesiastical policies

---

[27] Though unnecessary, as has been noted, the fact remains that spiritual vitality seldom follows an even course. Human nature being what it is, there seem to be periods of lifelessness, times when there is only a halting response to the Spirit's appeals; then after a period of lethargy, there may come awakening in newness of life. James Burns notes that the Psalms are a good example of this variation in spiritual sensitivity. At one time the writer, caught up by an inflowing wave of blessing, "exults in his strength, his heart rejoices in God, though a host should encamp against him, he shall not be afraid. But this jubilant note does not last; soon, caught in the trough of the wave, his voice cries out for help, his heart is in despair, light and hope alike seem to have forsaken him. From this he is rescued by the hand of the Lord, and carried forward in a new tide of joyful, spiritual experience." Mr. Burns observes that this fluctuation in experience actually serves to call our attention to the work of God. In fact, he believes there would be the possibility of taking God's life for granted were it not for these cycles of depression and exaltation. James Burns, *op. cit.*, pp. 26, 27.

of the church, revival fires still burned in the hearts of a faithful remnant and from time to time this smoldering flame would burst forth. There were seasons of refreshing under such leaders as Augustine in the early fifth century, Justinian and Gregory in the middle and late sixth century, and John of Damascus in the early eighth century. During the dark Middle Ages the cause of revival was kept alive in such movements as those gathered around Bernard of Clairvaux in the eleventh century, Francis of Assisi and Peter Waldo in the early thirteenth century, John Towle and John Wycliffe in the early fourteenth century, and Savonarola in the late fifteenth century.

The Protestant Reformation was a new revival conflagration calling the church back to God and the Bible. The Anabaptists especially deserve recognition for their fervent spirit of evangelism, which blazed a trail of heartfelt religion across Europe. When the Church became embroiled with scholastic disputation, the pietistic and later the Wesleyan revivals served to breathe new life upon the dead bones. From these revivals missionaries scattered out over the world and in many areas the churches which they established have experienced great outpourings of the Spirit.

OUR AMERICAN HERITAGE

To a remarkable degree, revivals have molded the course of the church in America.[28] Peter G. Mode of the University

---

[28] The course of these revivals and their effect upon the century has been treated by many historians. Some of the more popular general works are: F. G. Beardsley, *A History of American Revivals* (New York: American Tract Society, 1904); W. A. Candler, *Great Revivals and the Great Republic* (Nashville: Methodist Publishing House, 1904); Benjamin Rice Lacy, *Revivals in the Midst of the Years* (Richmond: John Knox Press, 1943); W. L. Muncy, *A History of Evangelism in the United States* (Kansas City: Central Seminary Press, 1945); and Bernard A. Weisberger, *They Gathered at the River* (Boston: Little, Brown, 1958). Further bibliographic information on revival may be found in Gerald Ira Gingrich's *Protestant Revival Yesterday and Today* (New York: Exposition Press, 1959), pp. 103–114.

of Chicago says that "more than any other phenomenon, they have supplied the landmarks of our religious history." [29] William Warren Sweet, dean of American church historians, has characterized these revivals as "cascades in the stream of the church, recreating the main course of its waters." [30] Were it not for these seasons of refreshing during several crucial periods when the very existence of the Republic was in jeopardy, it is doubtful if our country could have survived.

Unfortunately, in recent years, the experience of revival has declined. Many true disciples of Christ have kept the reality alive, and from time to time in scattered local areas there have been some general outpourings of the Spirit. Nevertheless, there has been no real national awakening in more than a century. Historically we cannot expect to drift much longer. If revival does not come in our generation, there is little hope for the next. We are at the crossroads now.

GOD IS ABLE

Years ago, after the funeral of General William Booth of the Salvation Army, the sexton found a lone Methodist preacher on his knees at the altar. Still thinking of the tremendous impact of the life of this one man upon the world, the preacher was overheard to say: "O Lord, do it again! Lord, do it again!"

As you think about the great times of revival in the past, and then consider the desperate situation today, do you not find yourself also praying that God will do it again, that men will come forth who will believe God for the impossible and that their numbers will increase until a new and mighty demonstration of holy love sweeps across the land? God grant that it may be so! "Lord, will Thou not revive us again that Thy people may rejoice in Thee."

---

[29] Peter G. Mode, *The Frontier Spirit in American Christianity* (New York: Macmillan, 1923), p. 41.

[30] William Warren Sweet, *Revivalism in America* (New York: Charles Scribner's Sons, 1944), p. xv.

STUDY ASSIGNMENTS

1

PERSONAL STUDY

The following questions for thought are intended to help you get a Biblical perspective of the lesson and to make some personal applications. You may want to take a question or two during your private devotions each day. Normally a lesson can be completed in a week, although you may want to extend the time on some of the later lessons. It is suggested that you use a small notebook to record your answers.

1. Meditate upon Psalms 80:18; 85:6 and 138:7. Write in a sentence your understanding of what revival means in these passages.

2. Where is the source of this spiritual life? Note Isaiah 57:15 and Deuteronomy 6:24; 32:39.

3. What is the blessing of revival described in Hosea 6:1–3 and 14:7?

4. One of the great revivals of the Bible occurred during the reign of King Hezekiah. Read the account of this period in II Chronicles 29:1–32:31. List some of the blessings that accompanied this revival, noting the Biblical references.

   Why was Hezekiah a worthy leader of revival? II Chronicles 31:21 (29:2).

5. As you interpret revival in terms of your own personal situation, can you see some areas where you believe the experience of victorious Christianity can be enlarged in your life? Note three.

6. How do you feel that your church can experience revival?

7. What would be the effect of real revival in your community?

8. Write out in your own words the prayer of Habakkuk 3:2. Preserve the spirit of the prayer, yet phrase it in terms appropriate to your situation.

GROUP DISCUSSION

After you have completed the personal study, discuss your ideas with a group of people who share your same concern. You may get together at stated times outside the regular church schedule, or if this is not convenient, meet during the regular service of your prayer meeting, Sunday school or evening worship. Six to eight people make up a good group, though you may have a few more. Whether you meet as couples or individuals does not matter, but it is wise to keep generally within the same age level.

One person can be designated as the leader of the group. If you desire, this leadership can be rotated each week. The leader is responsible for keeping the discussion alive and to draw out the participation of each member of the group. A good procedure is to ask questions which call for a definite personal opinion, such as "John, what does this mean to you?" When a question arises within the group, the leader may refer it to another person, for example, "Jim, how would you answer John's question?"

The groups should plan to meet from forty-five minutes to an hour, depending upon the circumstances. Usually the first part of the period is given to sharing insights gained in personal study. The latter part should be a time of prayer, remembering especially needs which have been expressed during the meeting. And don't forget to praise God.

For this first meeting, let each one read his definition of revival from question 1. Then some can give their answers to questions 2 through 4. If you care to mention it to the group, answers to questions 5 through 7 can be read. After this, let each person tell the most memorable experience of revival in the church which can be recalled. Be perfectly free in expressing your views. To conclude the time together, some can read the prayer recorded in question 8.

2 - Conditions for Revival

Since revival is the work of God, the question might be asked: Why is it delayed? Surely the compassions of the Lord fail not. Then in the light of our great need, why does not revival come? This is a question which each of us must honestly raise.

GOD SETS CONDITIONS

Some cast the responsibility for revival completely upon God. The idea is that man can do nothing about it, and therefore we must simply wait upon the Lord. This view correctly emphasizes the absolute sovereignty of God, but when it is made an excuse for our indifference to the moral obligations of His law, then this truth is taken out of context.

Certainly revivals are Godsent. As a display of sovereign grace, they are entirely supernatural in their source and strength. Yet we must also realize that God does not violate His own integrity in sending them. The mighty power by which He breaks through human impotence is consistent with His Word. Revivals are given by God when His will is done by man.

This does not mean for a moment that spiritual awakening is the hip hip hurray of human activity, as if it can be "worked up" by something we do. It merely underscores the necessity for human response to divine action. God is no respecter of persons but He is a respecter of conditions.

Where God's conditions are met we can be confident that revival will come. As Charles G. Finney put it: "Revival is the right use of the appropriate means. The means which God has enjoined . . . produce revival. Otherwise God would not have enjoined them." [1] Hence, "if we need to be revived, it is our duty to be revived. If it is our duty, it is possible." [2] Billy Graham stresses the same principle when he says: "I believe that we can have revival anytime we meet God's conditions. I believe that God is true to His Word and that He will rain righteousness upon us if we meet His conditions." [3]

This conclusion is only logical since God always wants the best for His people. When the Spirit of revival does not prevail, it is purely a human failure to exercise God-given privileges of grace. Never can a thrice Holy God be held responsible for the degenerate condition of the world or the church.

It is not a question then of God's ability or desire to send revival. The question is: Do we want God's will to be done? If we dare say "Yes," then we commit ourselves to remove any

---

[1] Charles G. Finney, *op. cit.*, p. 5. Many people have taken exception to Finney's view of revival because he said that it was not a miracle in the sense that the laws of nature were suspended. However, in making these statements, Finney did not mean that revivals were naturalistic in the sense that man brought them to pass. In his reaction to extreme Calvinism, Finney was merely trying to emphasize the imperative of human responsibility in using the means provided by God. "But means," he said "will not produce a revival, we all know, without the blessing of God. It is impossible for us to say that there is not as direct an influence or agency from God, to produce a crop of grain, as there is to produce a revival. . . . A revival is as naturally a result of the use of the appropriate means as a crop is of the use of its appropriate means."
[2] *Ibid.*, pp. 33, 34.
[3] Billy Graham, "We Need Revival," *Revival in Our Time* (Wheaton: Van Kampen Press, 1950), pp. 76, 77.

impediment in our lives that would hinder revival, and furthermore, we obligate ourselves to do it now. God's will is clear. The next move is up to us.

THE AUTHORITY OF GOD'S WORD

Underlying this whole concern, of course, is the recognition of divine authority. There is no point talking about revival unless we believe that God means business. "If my people, which are called by my name, shall humble themselves, and pray, and seek my face, and turn from their wicked ways; then will I hear from heaven, and will forgive their sin, and will heal their land" (II Chronicles 7:14). Again He promises: "But if from thence thou shalt seek the Lord thy God, thou shalt find him, if thou shalt seek him with all thy heart and with all thy soul" (Deuteronomy 4:29).

When we are willing to line up with God's Word, there is no limit to His blessing. ". . . Prove me now herewith, saith the Lord of hosts, if I will not open you the windows of heaven, and pour you out a blessing, that there shall not be room enough to receive it" (Malachi 3:10). ". . . The Lord will give grace and glory: no good thing will He withhold from them that walk uprightly" (Psalm 84:11). A thousand other promises declare the same provision. God is always for us. If we who are evil know how to give good things to our children, how much more will our Father in heaven "give the Holy Spirit to them that ask Him" (Luke 11:13). Why then should anyone struggle on in spiritual defeat when all the resources of grace are available to the obedient heart?

Do we really believe what God says? This is a question that must be voiced at the beginning, for everything else depends upon our response. Obviously, if there is some doubt about the trustworthiness of God's revealed Word, there is likely to be little concern to measure our life by it. Systems of thought which discredit the Holy Scripture never produce revival.

Let us be clear at this point. The Bible is not incidental to revival.[4] As the eternal Book of God, it is the objective authority for all that we believe and practice. Apart from its immutable truth, standards of justice and holiness would degenerate into little more than whims of public opinion. Even the Revelation of Christ, the living Word of God, would be lost in confusion and uncertainty if it were not for the unwavering testimony of Scripture. In this light, the Bible, and the Bible alone, is our basis for determining what to believe, the instrument of all divine blessing, the means through which the Holy Spirit ministers to our yearning hearts the grace of God.

Submission to this authority is the first requirement for revival. God has sent forth His Word that unto Him every knee should bow (Isaiah 45:23). When God speaks, we must listen. It is not our place to change or minimize the message. Nor are we called to defend what God says. The Bible is not on trial; we are. Our place is only to trust and obey. Once this is settled, our hearts are open for spiritual instruction.

CONFESSION OF SIN

The Word gives us an authority for our faith, but it also makes us face ourselves before the refining eyes of God's holiness. We see ourselves in the light of Jesus Christ. In His sight our righteousness is as filthy rags. The props of self-sufficiency are knocked out from under our pride. We are found out for what we are—sinners.

---

[4] A discussion of this principle in the history of the Church is A. M. Chirgiven's *The Bible in World Evangelism* (New York: Friendship Press, 1954). One of the more recent illustrations of this is the Indonesian revival today, one of the great spiritual movements of our time. Already more than a quarter of a million people have been brought to Christ through the witness of this revival, and the work is still going on. For an account of how it started with a little boy who brought home a New Testament and began to read it to his family, see the article by Stanley Mooneyham, "Indonesia: From Slumber to Revival," *Decision*, VIII, 12, Dec. 1967, pp. 3, 13.

As the dreadful sense of guilt increases, the awful realization of impending judgment deepens. A holy fear grips our hearts, and we may be left with a feeling of utter helplessness. There is no place to hide from God.

One thing is certain. When the Spirit truly convicts our souls, however it may be felt, sin cannot be treated with indifference. Frivolity and lightheartedness are gone. We do not have to be urged to flee from the wrath to come. When we are broken and contrite in spirit, our hearts are disposed to heed any offer of mercy. Begging men to come to Christ may be necessary in an atmosphere of complacency, but in the throes of revival "sinners beg Christ to receive them." [5]

Once we have been awakened to our need, we must do something about it. Conviction of sin leads to repentance. There can be no revival until we confess our sin, turn from our evil ways, and throw ourselves upon the mercy of the Lord. "If I regard iniquity in my heart, the Lord will not hear me" (Psalms 66:18).

Any impediment to the flow of God's grace must be removed. Unbelief, lust, lying, cheating, unclean thoughts, filthy speech, dirty habits, cursing, ingratitude, indifference to responsibility, disregard of self-discipline, prayerlessness, robbing God of tithes, neglect of the poor, racial discrimination, an unforgiving spirit, backbiting, envy, jealousy, bitterness, deceitfulness, selfishness, hypocrisy—whatever it is, whether it be a deed or a disposition, if known to be contrary to the holiness of God, it must be confessed and forsaken. [6]

There can be no compromise. Repentence is a thorough

---

[5] C. E. Autrey, *Revivals of the Old Testament* (Grand Rapids: Zondervan, 1960), p. 21. A moving description of conviction in revival may be found in Oswald J. Smith's *The Revival We Need* (London: Marshall, Morgan and Scott, 1940), pp. 45–56.

[6] For a searching inventory of sins common among Christians, read Horatius Bonar's *Words to Winners of Souls* (Oradell, New Jersey: American Tract Society, reprint, 1962). One can scarcely read this little book without falling on his knees.

housecleaning. As far as we are concerned, there is a complete turning from sin. Not only must confession be made to God, but we must be willing to do all we can to make things right with people we have wronged. If we try to trim the corners, and excuse a few favorite shortcomings, we are fooling ourselves. No revival can come in our hearts until sin is out of the way. Furthermore, until this is true of our lives, we stand in the way of God's blessing to others.

The great revival that came to the New Hebrides Islands in 1949 is a splendid example. Led by their minister, a little group of earnest Christians entered into a covenant with God that they would "give Him no rest until He had made Jerusalem a praise in the earth." Months passed, but nothing happened. Then one night a young man arose from his knees and read from Psalm 24: "Who shall ascend unto the hill of the Lord? or who shall stand in his holy place? He that hath clean hands and a pure heart. . . . He shall receive the blessing from the Lord . . ." (vs. 3–5). The young man closed his Bible, and looking at his companions on their knees, said: "Brethren, it is just so much humbug to be waiting thus night after night, month after month, if we ourselves are not right with God. I must ask myself, 'Is my heart pure? Are my hands clean?'" [7]

As the men faced this question, they fell on their faces in confession and consecration. That night revival came to the town. The whole community was shaken by the power of God, and within a few weeks the revival had moved across the island sweeping literally thousands of people into the Kingdom.

So every revival begins. God can use a small vessel, but He will not use a dirty one. An Achan in the camp will always have an influence for evil upon many others. Let us be sure that our hearts are clean. "Search me, O God, and

---

[7] Reported by Duncan Campbell, leader of this revival, as quoted in Arthur Wallis, *op. cit.*, p. 124.

know my heart; try me, and know my thoughts: And see if there be any wicked way in me . . ." (Psalms 139:23, 24).

PREVAILING PRAYER

When the channel is clean, the Spirit of God can flow through the believing heart in true intercessory prayer.[8] Such prayer is wrought from hearts overwhelmed with the sense of unworthiness yet captivated by the knowledge of God's forgiving grace. At first our cries for help may be faltering, but as the burden increases in intensity and scope, prayer becomes focused on the real need.

When revival was sweeping through Wales in 1904 a man who visited one of the meetings stood up and asked: "Friends, I have journeyed into Wales with the hope that I may glean the secret of the Welsh revival." Instantly, Evan Roberts, leader of the revival, was on his feet, and with an uplifted arm toward the speaker, replied: "My brother, there is no secret: Ask and ye shall receive!" [9]

That's it! Revival comes when God's people prevail in prayer.[10] "As soon as Zion travailed, she brought forth her

---

[8] The cleansing which we receive through the blood of Christ enables us to assume the role of a priest before God, and our ministry in this capacity finds its highest expression in prayer for others. Hence the whole purpose of redemption while we live on this earth culminates in intercession. A forceful and concise statement on this subject is the book by Lewis Sperry Chafer, *True Evangelism* (London: Marshall, Morgan and Scott, 1919). As Dr. Chafer puts it, "The personal element in true soul-winning work is more a work of pleading *for* souls than a service of pleading *with* souls. It is talking with God about men from a clean heart and in the power of the Spirit, rather than talking to men about God," p. 93. This idea is also developed in S. D. Gordon's *Quiet Talks on Prayer* (New York: Grosset & Dunlap, 1941), pp. 7–70.

[9] Quoted from an unpublished account of the Welsh Revival by Arthur Walles, *op. cit.,* p. 112.

[10] An excellent treatment of this subject may be found in Charles G. Finney, *op. cit.,* pp. 49–114. His lectures recorded here on "Prevailing Prayer," "The Prayer of Faith" and "The Spirit of Prayer" reflect the passion of one who believed that God always grants the request of a true prayer of faith. A more recent appeal for such praying is the stirring book by Leonard Ravenhill, *Revival Praying* (Minneapolis: Bethany Fellowship, 1962).

children." Jesus has promised: ". . . whatsoever ye shall ask in my Name, that will I do. . . . If ye shall ask anything in my Name, I will do it" (John 14:13, 14, cf., 15:7, 16; 16:23–26). The "Name" of Jesus, of course, is just another way of expressing the person and work of the Master. To pray in His Name is to pray in His character, to pray in His Spirit, to pray as Jesus Himself is praying as Mediator before the Father.

Seen this way, prayer implies our complete identification with the purpose of God. Jesus called out, in the inner depth of human emptiness, ". . . not my will, but thine, be done" (Luke 22:42, cf., Matthew 26:39; Mark 14:36). His prayer was not passive submission to the Father, but a determined plea that God's will would prevail over all else. Prayer has its joys, and it always throbs with thanksgiving, but supremely it is seen in Jesus to be active conformity to the will of God.

Where this condition is fulfilled, nothing is impossible (I John 5:14, 15). Whatever limits are imposed upon the power of prayer are entirely of our own making. We can go through all the forms of prayer, but until we actually want God's will to be done more than we want life itself, we are not in the Spirit of prayer.

Such praying is never easy. It will make us face the cross. It will mean deep searching of soul and real sacrifice. When Jesus prayed in Gethsemane the burden of His mission was so great upon His heart that while He prayed ". . . his sweat was as it were great drops of blood falling down upon the ground" (Luke 22:44). Prayer was indeed the sweat, tears, and blood of His ministry (Hebrews 5:7). Everything else was easy in comparison to His intercession before the throne of God. The battle of Calvary was fought and won in prayer.

THE WAY OF CONQUEST

So it is with every victory of grace. The weapons of this warfare are not fleshly, but are "mighty through God to the pulling down of strong holds" (II Corinthians 10:4). As

Sidlow Baxter has put it, "men may spurn our appeals, reject our message, oppose our arguments, despise our persons—but they are helpless against our prayers." [11] Satan has already defeated us if we try any substitute. Believing, persistent, determined prayer is the only way of victory. We can do more than pray after we have prayed, the godly A. J. Gordon has reminded us, "but we cannot do more than pray until we have prayed." [12]

A little group of praying Christian businessmen in Charlotte, North Carolina, illustrate this principle so well. During the depression of 1932 they became greatly concerned about the spiritual and moral decay in their city.[13] Believing that the situation called for an all-out evangelistic effort, they asked the Ministerial Association to undertake a united Crusade, assuring the clergy of their support. However, the ministers, somewhat skeptical of this type of meeting, declined the request.

Though disappointed, the laymen still felt that God wanted to do something big in their city, and not knowing what else to do, they decided to call for a day of prayer. All who could were asked to come to a quiet, wooded spot on the outskirts of Charlotte and spend the day waiting upon the Lord. Twenty-nine persons responded to that first invitation. As they fasted and prayed, the faith of the men grew stronger. They prayed that God would be pleased to send a revival to their city and that it would spread over the state and out to the ends of the earth. This time proved such a blessing that in the months following similar meetings were called.

---

[11] Sidlow Baxter, quoted by Cameron V. Thompson, *Master Secrets of Prayer* (Guatemala: Service of Life Schools), p. 4.

[12] A. J. Gordon, *op. cit.*, p. 18.

[13] An account of this laymen's group is given by Edward E. Ham in *The Story of an All-day Prayer Meeting and the Revival When Billy Graham Found Christ* (Wheaton: Sword of the Lord Publishers, 1955). It is also alluded to in the biography by John Pollock, *Billy Graham* (New York: McGraw-Hill Book Co., 1966), pp. 5, 6; and William G. McLoughlin, Jr.'s *Billy Graham* (New York: Ronald Press, 1960), pp. 27–29.

Two of these were held on the farm of W. Frank Graham, a dairyman and devout churchman, who shared the men's concern for revival. Particularly was he burdened for one of his own children, William, a teen-age boy who needed to come to grips with God.

Out of these repeated times of prayer the men felt led to sponsor an evangelistic meeting in the city. Accordingly they purchased a small tent and set it up for Gospel services in the summer of 1933. This effort was so encouraging that the men decided to undertake a much larger crusade the following year. The Reverend Mordecai Ham was invited to preach. Many difficulties were encountered in getting ready for the meeting, and several times it seemed as if it would never materialize, but the men persisted in their prayers and labors, and finally in the fall of 1934 the Charlotte Crusade began.

What happened in that meeting is now well known. For it was there that the young boy Billy Graham, along with many others, was converted. A spirit was ignited in his life which has blazed a trail for God around the world. Yet when I see the tremendous ministry of this great evangelist, and thrill at the way God has used him to challenge so many today with the claims of Christ, I cannot help but think of that little group of earnest Christian laymen, along with Billy's dad, down on their knees in the piney woods of North Carolina imploring God to show His omnipotence in a new way.

That is the way revival begins. It always starts in a prayer meeting as we seek first the Kingdom and commit our lives for God to use as He pleases. When we truly take sides with heaven, and pray with Christ, inevitably there will be fruit (John 15:1–17).

BEARING THE CROSS

One thing more needs to be stressed. Prayer leads to action. We cannot expect God to pour out his blessing upon the world unless we are willing to become involved in some kind of redemptive service. The yielding of our lives to the Spirit's control means that we must make ourselves available for God to use in answering our prayers.

Whatever the form our service might take, at its heart will be evangelism—the labor of love bringing all men by all means to know the Christ whom to know aright is life everlasting. If we are not occupied by this concern, we are a contradiction to the Spirit of our loving Lord who came "to seek and to save that which was lost" (Luke 19:10). It is silly to talk about going all the way with Christ when we are neglecting the work to which He gave His life.

An atheist once wrote in derision:

> Did I firmly believe, as millions say they do, that the knowledge and practice of religion in this life influences destiny in another . . . I should esteem one soul gained for heaven worth a life of suffering. Earthly consequences should never stay my hand, nor seal my lips. Earth, its joys and its griefs, would occupy no moment of my thoughts. I would strive to look upon eternity alone and on the immortal souls around me, soon to be everlastingly happy or everlastingly miserable. I would go forth to the world and preach it in season and out of season, and my text would be "what shall it profit a man if he gain the whole world and lose his soul?" [14]

A young, wealthy, carefree cricket player in England read these words, and though he tried to dismiss them, he could not escape their challenge to his Christian indifference. Finally sheer honesty brought C. T. Studd to his knees, and he made a full commitment to Christ. Giving up his fortune, he became a missionary spreading seeds of revival across two continents. When people wondered why he spared not himself in his

---

[14] Quoted in Norman Grubb, *C. T. Studd* (Atlantic City, N. J.: World Wide Prayer Movement, 1935), p. 40.

passion to get the Gospel to those who had not heard, he replied: "If Jesus be God and died for me, then no sacrifice can be too great for me to make for Him." [15]

Isn't this really what it means to bear the cross of Christ (Mark 8:34; Matthew 10:38; 16:24)? The cross is not a physical infirmity nor is it some difficult problem of our environment, as some people suppose. The cross is where Jesus freely gave His life for our redemption. Its purpose centered in evangelism. When we embrace the cross as our way of life, do we then not commit ourselves to the purpose for which Christ bore the cross for us?

Here finally is where we must face the issue. It is well enough for us in the church to sing about the cross on which the Prince of glory died, but what is more to the point is for us to come down in the affairs of this world and take up that cross ourselves. In practical terms, this means that we must offer our bodies in living dedication to His ministry of reconciliation. "Without this giving of ourselves to serve those Christ loved and died to save, our spiritual experience is not likely to mean much to the world or to the church." [16]

ENABLED BY HIS SPIRIT

Jesus prayed that this sense of mission would captivate the allegiance of His disciples. Just as He had dedicated Himself "for their sake," so also He prayed that they might be sanctified by the Spirit (John 17:18, 19).[17] Through their

---

[15] C. T. Studd, quoted in "A Sure Foundation," *Worldwide,* March–April, 1964.

[16] Taken from my paper read at the World Congress on Evangelism in Berlin, published in *One Race, One Gospel, One Task,* Vol. II, *op. cit.,* pp. 210–212.

[17] Sanctification means "to set apart" for God and hence to make holy. The context determines how the word is to be applied. In this instance, it relates to the preparation necessary for the fulfillment of Christ's mission in the world. The work of the Spirit in the lives of the disciples is to make them a blessing to the world. As Paul put it: ". . . meet for the Master's use, and prepared unto every good work" (II Timothy 2:21). For further discussion of the ministry of the Holy Spirit in a

witness, and in turn through the witness of those they won, Christ visualized how the world might believe in Him (John 17:20, 21). The fruitfulness of His ministry, indeed, the fulfillment of His whole incarnate life, death, and resurrection, depended upon their faithfulness to this commission. Had they been unwilling to accept the challenge and remained self-centered, the world would never have known the Gospel, and we would be lost without hope today.

Would that we could see this dimension of holiness in our lives! Many of us spend so much energy cultivating our piety that we make it a substitute for active evangelism. We get so wrapped up in our worship exercises, deeper life conventions, and sometimes even our meetings for revival, that we have no time nor energy for real soul-winning. Certainly we must feed our souls by Bible study and spiritual meditation, but spiritual indigestion will likely occur if this devotion does not find an outlet in practical service.

I am reminded of Charles Spurgeon's comment after reading the following passage: "And there came a messenger unto Job, and said, The oxen were plowing, and the asses feeding beside them."

"Yes," he said, lifting his eyes with a kindly glance around the crowded gallery, "that is still the case. Some of us are always plowing, breaking up the fallow ground, preparing the ground for good seed. And others are feeding. I know some of you dear people. You would not miss a service if you could help it. Feeding, everlasting feeding. It is good to feed, it is necessary to feed, but do a bit of Gospel plowing as well, for the health of your souls and the glory of God. The oxen were plowing, but the asses were feeding!" [18]

---

simple Bible study, see *The Spirit and the Word* (Huntington Valley, Pa.: Christian Outreach, 1968).

[18] Charles Spurgeon, quoted in *Worldwide*, Jan.–Feb., 1959, p. 7.

THE ISSUE MUST BE FACED

The disciples spent nearly three years feeding as they traveled with Jesus. There were times when they did some plowing, as when their Lord sent them out two by two to witness, but for the most part they seemed content just to enjoy their fellowship with Jesus. But if they were ever to be much use to the Kingdom, they needed to become involved much deeper in the work of Christ. Merely having their names written in the Book of Life was not enough to bring revival to others. They needed to come to grips with the real heartbreak of a lost world and show the wandering multitudes that there was One who cared. Every deep seated ambition and secret pride at cross purposes with God's program had to be crucified. In that utter emptiness of complete consecration they had to tarry until the reality of Christ's Presence filled their lives with His love and obedience. Then they could go forth in power as witnesses to the world. There was no use trying to get by on less. God promised them the fullness of His Spirit, and there could be no real revival without it.

Even so it is with us today. We, too, must look to the source of our life and, through the mighty power of the Holy Spirit, experience what it means to love God with all of our hearts, minds and strength, and to love our neighbors as ourselves. Nothing else will suffice.

Make no mistake about it! The responsibility for revival rests with us. Moreover, the conditions are clear. We must lay hold upon the surety of God's Word. We must confess our sin and turn from our deceitful ways. We must pray in the faith that God answers according to His will. And putting our lives at His disposal, we must work to bring men to Christ, counting not the cost. These conditions are merely different ways of saying the same thing, namely, that Christ must be exalted on earth as He is in heaven. When this condition exists, there is revival.

STUDY
ASSIGNMENTS
2

PERSONAL STUDY

1. Conditions for revival are listed in II Chronicles 7:14. After thinking through this verse, write it out in your own words, using contemporary language.

2. Condense to a sentence the condition for revival as proclaimed in Joshua 24:14, 15.

3. Read the account of revival in I Samuel 7:1–17. What was the secret of this season of refreshing? Note especially verse 3.

4. Read the record of revival under Asa in II Chronicles 14:1–15:19. How would you sum up the condition for God's continuous blessing according to 15:2?

5. Read the account of revival under the leadership of Josiah in II Chronicles 34:1–35:27. Why was Josiah qualified to be a leader to his people?

   What brought the king and the nation to face up to God's expectations?

6. Study the lesson on fruit bearing in John 15:1–17. What is the fundamental condition for bringing forth fruit? Note verses 4 and 5.

   How does the life of Christ enter you? Note verses 3, 7 and 10.

   What privilege does fruitfulness (abiding in Christ) give you? Note verses 7 and 16.

What is the supreme demonstration of Christ living in you? Note verses 9, 10, 12–14, 17.

Spiritually speaking, what do you think pruning means; and why does God prune branches in His vine? Note verse 2.

7. Why do you believe Jesus linked His sanctification with His mission to a lost world, as noted in John 17:18–20.

8. What does bearing the cross mean to you?

As you think about it, is there something more that you can do to make your cross more real? Specifically, what?

GROUP DISCUSSION

Following the same pattern of meeting as before, designate someone to lead the group. Be sure that everyone is acquainted. To start the discussion, one or two people can read their paraphrases of II Chronicles 7:14. Then move to question 2, letting someone read a summary statement. This procedure can be followed on through the other questions, allowing for discussion as there is need. If time starts to get away from you, go on to the last question where the personal application is made. Each person might be asked to sum up what he feels to be the greatest need in his life. These personal concerns, along with the general burdens of the church, can be made a subject of prayer in closing.

3 - Pattern of Revival in the Bible

Revival shapes the redemptive activity of the Holy Spirit throughout the Bible. Tracing this stream of life is like listening to man's heartbeat; it sounds the deep craving of man which will rise to assert itself when given a chance. But is there a discernible pattern in this witness of spiritual life, particularly in relation to the masses? A broad review of the inspired narrative will help us answer this question.[1]

EARLY LESSONS ABOUT REVIVAL

The story of revival begins with the Genesis history. Perhaps what might be called the first general awakening occurred in the days of Seth, shortly after the birth of his son Enos, when

---

[1] While no amount of reading in other sources can substitute for a direct confrontation with the Scripture itself, the student may find it helpful to consult secondary materials where available. Seven of the Old Testament revivals are treated by C. E. Autrey in *Revivals of the Old Testament, op. cit.* Both Old and New Testament revivals are considered in less detail by Ernest Baker in *Great Revivals of the Bible* (London: The Kingsgate Press, 1906). There are also some selected studies available, such as Wilbur M. Smith's little book, *The Glorious Revival Under King Hezekiah* (Grand Rapids: Zondervan, 1954). Of course, commentaries and histories of the two Testaments will allude to revivals in the course of their interpretation of Scripture, and sometimes these accounts are rich with insights; however, the need is apparent for more scholarly and creative work in this area, and a definitive study has yet to be written.

46

it is said that ". . . then began men to call upon the name of the Lord" (Genesis 4:26).

Significantly the word "Enos" means feeble or sickly. When it is recalled that this account follows the murder of Abel (Genesis 3:9-15), as well as the growing evidence of disease in the human race, one can easily see why such a name was appropriate. Probably it reflects an awareness of man's depravity and need for grace.

Apart from this one allusion, however, there is no record of any great mass awakening in the early history of Adam's race. Men lived long in those days, and their families were prolific, but with the exception of Enoch, there does not seem to be any corresponding fruitfulness in the things of God. This may explain why conditions in the world eventually deteriorated to the point that "the Lord [was sorry] that He had made man on the earth" (Genesis 6:6).

The subsequent account of the deluge of the world by the flood dramatically illustrates what happens to a sinful people when the call to revival is unheeded (Genesis 6:1-7:22). Noah, "a just man and perfect in his generation" (Genesis 6:9), is said to be a "preacher of righteousness" (II Peter 2:5), which suggests that he warned his generation of God's impending judgment. Though the Spirit sought to bring conviction to the rebellious people for a hundred and twenty years, it does not appear that they wanted to repent. Finally God gave them up to their own destruction.

Likewise, the wicked inhabitants of Sodom and Gomorrah scorned revival in their day. Abraham travailed with God on their behalf but not ten people were found who could meet the accepted condition of personal righteousness (Genesis 18:14-19).

It is noteworthy that in both of these incidents cited by Jesus as examples of God's judgment (Matthew 24:37-39; 10:15), ample warning was given before the final execution of justice. Certainly they are graphic reminders that though God is longsuffering in the face of backsliding, there comes a time when His patience is exhausted. Ultimately it is either revival or catastrophe. We can be grateful that during these fearful days of judgment there were some men like Noah and Abraham whose obedience to God was beyond reproach, and who thereby preserved a posterity for the Lord.

LEADERSHIP OF THE FATHERS

For several centuries the patriarchs gave leadership to God's people, and when spiritual vitality languished, they were the rallying force for renewal. The brief revival in Jacob's house is a good example (Genesis 35:1–15). In this instance, the shameful behavior of Jacob's children among the Shechemites had created a situation in which the house of Israel faced annihilation by an enraged confederation of all the inhabitants in the land (Genesis 34:1–31). Destruction seemed certain. But Jacob, the spokesman for God, rose to the occasion. He commanded that his household put away their strange gods, purify themselves and go back to Bethel, the place where before the blessing of the Lord had seemed so real. Though the repentance of his children was short-lived, and Jacob's own example rather careless (compare Genesis 35:4, 16), still it served to keep alive the chosen race.

However, the era of the godly Patriarchs runs its course. After the death of Joseph, no strong leadership comes forth to father the people, and with the passing of the friendly Pharoahs, the Israelites find themselves bereft of spiritual inspiration within and afflicted by cruel taskmasters without.

For hundreds of years the children of Israel languish in this bondage. Yet in their suffering, at last they remember God, their help in ages past. Somehow their tears turn into prayers, "and their cry came up unto God by reason of the bondage. And God heard their groaning, and God remembered his covenant with Abraham, with Isaac and with Jacob" (Exodus 2:23–24).

As usually happens in such situations, God answers prayer by raising up a shepherd for his people (Exodus 3:1–22). Under the leadership of Moses some exciting seasons of refreshing follow, particularly in the events surrounding the first Passover (Exodus 12:21–28), the giving of the Law at Sinai (Exodus 19:1–25; 24:1–8; 32:1–35:29), and the lifting up of the brazen serpent at Mount Hur (Numbers 21:4–9). But, as so often before, the people soon forget their vows and turn back on God. The only stabilizing influence in the nation is Moses and the few faithful men gathered around him.

PERIODIC AWAKENING IN THE NATION

As the ungrateful people perish in the wilderness, God raises up a new generation, and Joshua is called to lead them into the promised land. For the most part a spiritual enthusiasm pervades their campaigns, as in the crossing of the river Jordan (Joshua 3:1–5:12) and the conquest of Ai (Joshua 7:1–8:35). However, several years after the wars end, and the people settle down to enjoy the spoils of victory, a spiritual apathy creeps over the lulled nation. Knowing that many of his people are divided, Joshua gathers the tribes of Israel at Shechem and there demands that every man choose once and for all whom he will serve (Joshua 24:1–32). A real revival follows this challenge, which continues on "all the days of the elders that overlived Joshua, and which had known all the works of the Lord, that he had done for Israel" (Joshua 24:31).

The period of rule by the judges for the next three hundred years shows the Israelites again and again forsaking the Lord and serving other gods. Judgment inevitably follows, and after a long period of oppression, the people repent and cry to God for help (Judges 3:9, 15; 4:3; 6:6, 7; 10:10). Each time

God answers their prayer by sending a deliverer who leads the people in conquest of their enemy. The greatest of these movements comes at the close of the era under the judgeship of Samuel (I Samuel 7:1–17).

There are periodic times of renewal during the age of the Kings. David's march into Jerusalem with the Ark demonstrates many ingredients of spiritual awakening (II Samuel 6:12–23; I Chronicles 15:25–16:36). The dedication of the Temple in the early reign of Solomon approaches the same spirit (I Kings 8:1–65; II Chronicles 5:1–7:22). After the division of the kingdom, a gracious revival comes to Judah in the days of Asa (I Kings 15:9–15; II Chronicles 15:1–19). Jehoshophat leads a reformation in his time (I Kings 22:41–50; II Chronicles 17:1–21:1). Jehoida the priest sparks a revival during the first years of King Joash (II Kings 11:4–12:16; II Chronicles 23:1–24:22). A mighty awakening is savored in the land under the leadership of King Hezekiah (II Kings 18:1–8; II Chronicles 29:1–31:21). Finding the book of the law precipitates a revival in Josiah's rule (II Kings 22:1–23:30; II Chronicles 34:1–35:19).

It is interesting that all of these revivals center in the Southern Kingdom of Judah. The nearest thing to a national awakening among the Northern tribes comes at Mount Carmel when Elijah triumphs over the prophets of Baal (I Kings 18:1–46). This victory is short-lived and not repeated, which doubtless is a big reason why the beleaguered ten tribes crumble a hundred and fifty years sooner than the little kingdom to the South. Nevertheless, even in Judah conditions rapidly deteriorate following Josiah's reign, and when no revival comes to avert God's wrath, the children of Israel are conquered and carried away into captivity.

Bondage again brings the Jews to their knees, and God moves upon the pagan king of Persia to send a large contingent of the Israelites back to Jerusalem to rebuild the Temple. Under the leadership of Zerubbabel and Jeshua revival fires begin to burn (Ezra 1:1–4:24). When harassment causes the Jews to quit their task, the prophets Haggai and

Zechariah stir up the people to keep on (Ezra 5:1–6:22; Haggai 1:1–2:23; Zechariah 1:1–21; 8:1–23). Seventy-five years later, with the coming of another expedition to Judah led by Ezra, new reforms are initiated and more attention is given to the obligations of the law (Ezra 7:1–10:44). The revival reaches its climax a few years later when Nehemiah arrives to finish the building of the walls of Jerusalem and establishes a holy government (Nehemiah 1:1–13:31).

HOPE OF ISRAEL KEPT ALIVE

These periods of reformation through the Old Testament are the high peaks of corporate worship in the life of Israel. Though we might wish that they gave the Jews more compassion for others,[1] still the revivals served again and again to rally the chosen people around their own heritage of holiness.

Unfortunately, they usually lacked depth and permanence among the masses. In spite of many noble reforms, the renewal movements never seem to completely erase the tendency of rebellion in the nation.[2] It would appear that expediency more often than not dictates the people's choice. When religious devotion is expected of them by their leaders, the people comply; but when the pressure is off, they take the path of least resistance.

---

[1] Evangelism of the pagan world is not given emphasis in the Old Testament concept of revival. However, there is the story of Jonah's mission to Ninevah which results in something of an awakening in that heathen city (Jonah 1:1–4:11). Clearly from the beginning, God's compassion was not limited to the Jews. But for the sake of His purpose of world evangelism, the Spirit's work in the Old Testament narrows upon the nation through whom redemption will come.

[2] There is an undercurrent of rebellion all through the history of Israel (Jeremiah 3:25; 8:5; Zechariah 1:4–6; Acts 7:51–53). Revival times may check this condition, but it is still there to assert itself when given a chance (for example, note Isaiah 65:1–3 in reference to Hezekiah's reign, or Jeremiah 3:6–11 which alludes to Josiah's era). This may remind us of the law serving as a schoolmaster to bring us to Christ. It may also underscore the need for more depth in follow-up to popular movements of renewal.

The stream of real revival flows largely in the hearts of a few men who bear the burden of the Lord. Even in times of national apostasy, there is this faithful remnant who will not capitulate to evil. In their experience with God, they keep alive the hope of that special nation through which Immanuel will bring redemption to the world.

REVIVAL IN THE COMING OF JESUS

In the fullness of time the promised Saviour does appear. He lives for thirty years in relative obscurity. Then, as the time draws near for His public ministry to begin, suddenly there comes a mighty prophet calling upon the people to repent, and saying, "Prepare ye the way of the Lord . . . he that cometh after me is mightier than I, whose shoes I am not worthy to bear: he shall baptize you with the Holy Ghost and with fire" (Matthew 3:1–12; cf. Mark 1:3–8; Luke 3:3–17; John 1:6–8, 15–17). A revival, such as Israel had not seen in 400 years, begins to sweep across the land.

As the excitement reaches its height, Jesus appears in the midst of the awakening and is baptized at the hand of John. There He is identified by the prophet as "The Lamb of God, which taketh away the sin of the world" (John 1:29; cf., 1:36). There the voice of God is heard from heaven, saying, ". . . Thou art my beloved Son, in whom I am well pleased" (Mark 1:11; Matthew 3:17; Luke 3:22). There, too, Jesus finds His first disciples (John 1:34–42).

Having now accomplished its special purpose, the movement centered in John the Baptist fades away, while the ministry of Christ quickly moves into prominence. At this point one might have expected Jesus to have seized the opportunity to proclaim Himself king and to establish a rule of righteousness by decree. Certainly, the opportunity is ripe for a great popular revolution. The people were fed up with the oppressions of Rome. They were eager to have their stomachs full and their national pride satisfied.

Yet the movement which begins to gather around Jesus takes a different course. Contrary to the pattern seen so often before, the Son of God does not seek the immediate following of the masses. Rather, in His infinite understanding of the human problem, He concentrates His attention upon a few men who are destined to be the nucleus of a Spirit-filled church.

PROBLEM OF THE MULTITUDES

Of course, large crowds do attend His public services, sometimes numbering into the thousands (e.g., Mark 6:44; Matthew 14:4; Luke 9:14; John 6:10). He instructs them. He feeds them. He heals them. Indeed, His deeds of mercy are so genuine that "all men" clamor for His attention (John 3:26; cf., 11:47; 12:19). Once the people want to "take Him by force, to make Him a king" (John 6:15). The enthusiasm with which the masses greet Jesus certainly indicates that the fields are ripe for harvest, particularly in Galilee (Mark 1:14–6:9; Matthew 4:17–14:21; Luke 4:14–9:9), Samaria (John 4:1–47), and Perea (Luke 13:22–19:28).

Had Jesus given any encouragement to this popular sentiment among the multitudes, He easily could have enlisted a vast army of followers and taken the country by storm. He needed only to satisfy the fleshly appetites and curiosities of the people by His miraculous power, and He could have had the world at His feet. For the first time in history a great welfare state where everyone had everything he needed appeared to be within the realm of possibility.

But Jesus had a much greater objective in view. He had not come to gain the superficial support of the multitudes, however sincere it might be; He came to establish an eternal Kingdom of the Spirit and to build a church against which the gates of hell could not prevail. Doubtless that is why Jesus chose to concentrate His life upon developing character and depth of dedication in a relatively small group of men. He knew that before the Gospel could effect a lasting change in the world some men had to be raised up who could lead the multitudes in the things of God.[2]

What good would it have been to His ultimate purpose to have aroused a great mass following without laying a foundation to assure their spiritual nurture? Time and time again it had been demonstrated that the crowd was an easy prey to false gods when left without proper care. The masses were like sheep without a shepherd (Mark 6:34; Matthew 9:36; 14:14). They were willing to follow almost anyone that came along with some promise for their welfare, be it friend or foe. That was the tragedy of the hour—the noble aspirations of the people were easily excited by Jesus, but just as quickly thwarted by the cold religious establishment that controlled them (John 8:44; 9:39–41; 12:40; cf., Matthew 23:2–39).

THE MASTER'S PLAN

Jesus is a realist. He knows full well the fickleness of depraved human nature as well as the satanic forces of this world amassed against humanity, and in this knowledge He follows a plan that will meet the need. The opportunity for a great national awakening is present, but Jesus individually could not possibly give to all the people the personal care needed to nurture the fruit of revival. His plan is to raise up men who can do it for Him and imbue them with His life

---

[2] This whole section on Jesus' ministry is taken from my book, *The Master Plan of Evangelism* (Westwood, New Jersey: Fleming H. Revell, 1964), pages 22–35. Since I have considerably reduced the portion of the book dealing with this subject, and have generally changed the wording, quotation marks have not been used. However due acknowledgment is made to this larger published work which deals with the basic strategy of evangelism in the life of Christ. The principles of evangelism outlined in this book form the basis for much of my thinking about revival. I believe that the way Jesus went about His ministry in principle is the way that all of us should pattern our lives, and this includes our work for revival.

and vision. Though He does all He can to help the multitudes, He has to devote Himself primarily to training a few in order that the masses can at last be permanently helped.

It is this practical concern that characterizes His approach to revival and directs the church about Him. Revival in His ministry has much the same purpose as before, but its strategy of preservation is given a new emphasis. While He plants and cultivates seeds of revival in the present, He is always preparing a band of disciples to reap the harvest in generations to come.

His method of training this vanguard of His church is simply to draw them together around Himself.[3] He does not establish a formal school nor does He prescribe a creed which His disciples must profess. All He asks is for them to follow Him. His teaching is incarnated in His own Person. By following Him they know the truth, the way and the life. In His company the disciples learn what it means to live in God, and also how to communicate His life to man.

After three years ministering with His disciples, Jesus goes to the cross. But before He leaves them, He makes it clear that "another Comforter," one in quality like Himself, will come to take His place in their midst. Through His Power they will be enabled to continue the ministry which Christ had begun. Though the Spirit had always been at work in the world to accomplish God's purpose, Jesus promised that

---

[3] The principle of Jesus' strategy in training men in the context of a small spiritual family was not new with His ministry, for it was God's basic plan of nurture from the very beginning. In fact, the home preceded any formal institution of the Church. The formal institution of worship grew out of the home, but it was never intended to take over the responsibility of religious instruction which resided in the family. This was clearly enunciated by Moses in the law (Deuteronomy 4:9; 6:7; 21:19; 31:13). The responsibility to train up children by precept and example clearly rested upon the parents. However, it would appear that throughout the Old Testament the burden of spiritual development was largely transferred to the institutional forms. What Jesus did was to take the basic pattern of the home and incorporate it into the structure of His day by day teaching ministry.

in a measure hitherto unknown to His disciples, they will experience the Presence of Christ in their lives (John 14:1–16:33).

It is easy to see why Jesus expects His disciples to tarry until this promise is realized. How else could they fulfill the great commission? The evangels of His Church must be obsessed with their Lord. His compassion for a lost world and His dedication to the work of God must become a burning compulsion within them. This can only become a reality as they are filled with His Spirit. Having enunciated this truth clearly, the glorified Jesus ascends into heaven leaving His expectant disciples waiting for the promised outpouring (Luke 24:49–53; Acts 1:1–26).

REVIVAL AT PENTECOST

The mighty infilling of the Holy Spirit at Pentecost is the fruition of His ministry (Acts 2:1–47). It marks the beginning of a new era in the history of redemption. For three years He had been working for this day—the day when His church, trained by His example, assured by His life, would go forth in His name to proclaim the Gospel "unto the uttermost part of the earth" (Acts 1:8).

As the Spirit-anointed witnesses declare "the wonderful works of God" to all that would hear, the multitudes stand in dismay before them (Acts 2:6–13). When Peter explains what it is all about, and the people are invited to believe on Christ, about three thousand receive the word and are baptized in their faith (Acts 2:41). What is more, they continue to grow in the life of their new found Lord (Acts 2:42). Brotherly concern (Acts 2:44), generosity (Acts 2:45) and unity of spirit characterize their life together (Acts 2:46). The love of God fills their souls with praise (Acts 2:46, 47). Miracles happen (Acts 2:43). As the people look on in amazement, they can see that something has made a difference. God is real! ". . . And the Lord added to the church daily such as should be saved" (Acts 2:47).

What happens on the day of Pentecost is only a foretaste of that which is to come. The revival continues to spread across the city of Jerusalem. Daily—in the Temple, in the streets, and in every house—the Christians cease not to teach and preach Jesus Christ (Acts 5:42). "Great power" and "great grace is upon them all" (Acts 4:33). Before long thousands are converted, including many of the Jewish priests (Acts 4:4; 6:1, 7). Their faith is attested by works of love. Freely do they give of their substance to care for the poor (Acts 4:34–37). With the same compassion, they believe for the healing of the sick (Acts 3:1–11; 5:12–16). And within their fellowship there is a wonderful oneness of heart and soul (Acts 4:32; 5:12).

DIFFICULTIES OVERCOME

Yet they have their problems. There is a couple among them, Ananias and Sapphira, who are deceitful in their profession (Acts 5:1–10). Whenever this many people get together there are likely to be some who do not belong. But the way God judges these hypocrites only serves to draw the church closer together in holiness and to bring more people from the outside to believe on Christ (Acts 5:11–14).

There is the problem, too, of a few Greek-speaking widows who feel that they are being neglected by the Hebrews in the daily ministration. When this situation is brought to the attention of the apostles, they wisely call a congregational meeting to discuss the matter, and out of this they decide to institute the order of deacons to assist in the administration of the local church (Acts 6:1–6). Again the way the problem is handled enhances the reputation of the Christian community, and the number of disciples greatly multiplies in Jerusalem (Acts 6:7). Problems confronted by the Church

57

in the glow of revival are made stepping stones to greater spiritual progress.[4]

We must not assume, however, that the Christians have it easy. Most of the time they witness under the threat of punishment by the ruling aristocracy (Acts 4:1–31; 5:17–42). They are beaten. They are imprisoned. One of their leaders, Stephen, is stoned to death (Acts 6:8–7:60). Yet their adversities never restrain their zeal or temper their joy. In fact, they rejoice that they are counted worthy to suffer shame for Jesus' sake (Acts 5:41). The persecutions succeed only in scattering the revival across the land, for wherever the Christians flee they carry with them the Spirit of Pentecost (Acts 8:1–4; 11:19). Even the martyrdom of Stephen contributes to the conversion of Saul, the chief persecutor of the church (Acts 8:1; 9:1–31).

THE REVIVAL SPREADS

As the years move on, so the revival continues to spread. Not everything that happens can be reported, of course, but it is significant that the events which are selected show how the Spirit of revival attends each breakthrough of the Gospel into new regions. It moves into Samaria where the first congregation is raised up outside the Jewish nation (Acts

---

[4] A rapid increase in church membership, as happened in the Jerusalem church, invariably precipitates some problems. There is always the danger of some coming into the movement who are superficial in their commitment, as was evident with Ananias and Sapphira. Also, when numbers swell the size of a congregation, usually administrative functions are sorely taxed to keep up with the increased demands, as was the case with the murmuring widows. There were other problems, too, which later came up in the expansion of the work: the greed of Simon (Acts 8:9–24); the hesitancy of the church to forgive and accept the converted Saul (Acts 9:26); legalism (Acts 11:10–18; 15:1–35); friction between ministers (Acts 13:13; 15:36–40); and fear (Acts 21:12). Revival does not prevent all conflicts, but it does give spiritual stamina to overcome them. A helpful discussion of this matter is in C. E. Autrey, *Evangelism in the Acts* (Grand Rapids: Zondervan, 1964), pp. 43–78.

8:5–25).[5] The revival reaches into the house of Cornelius at Caesarea, which marks the beginning of the work among Gentile believers (Acts 10:1–11:18; 15:7–28).[6] The same Spirit brings together a congregation of both Jews and Gentiles at Antioch (Acts 11:19–30). As this church becomes well established, the Spirit speaks to their listening hearts and two of their staff are sent out as missionaries to the world (Acts 13:1–4). Thereafter the action shifts to the exploits of Paul as he bears the Gospel witness to the ends of the earth.

Following the leadership of the Holy Spirit, the missionaries begin work in a new city by going to the most likely place spiritually hungry people are gathered—usually the synagogue. There they present the claims of Christ and draw out those whom the Spirit has made responsive to the truth. From this nucleus a congregation is established and their own people trained for leadership. In turn the Christians in the city go out and evangelize the surrounding area until "the word of the Lord was published throughout all the region" (Acts 13:49; 19:20, 26; I Thessalonians 1:8, 9). The harvests at Antioch in Pisidia (Acts 13:14–52), Philippi (Acts 16:12–40), Thessalonica (Acts 17:1–9; I Thessalonians 1:8, 9) and Ephesus (Acts 18:19–19:41; 20:17–38) are especially interesting to study.

The story reads like one long narrative of Pentecost. Nothing can stop them—not the anger of mobs or the irritations of

---

[5] Perhaps it is worthy of note that the first penetration of the Gospel outside the Jewish world of that day comes in the same area where a few years before there had been a remarkable response to Jesus' ministry (John 4:39–42). Doubtless the message of Christ was not altogether new to these people, and very likely there were already some in the area who were believers. We cannot help but observe the principle of beginning where there is the greatest spiritual preparation.

[6] Again we note the pattern of beginning with those whose hearts are already yearning for spiritual reality. Cornelius and his house were probably the most sensitive people in the Gentile world at that time. Though their understanding of truth was limited, still they were walking in all the light they had, and when they received the more complete Revelation through the Apostle, their hearts were immediately responsive.

daily trials, but as rivers borne along with a loud rushing sound, they go on their way praising God and scattering abroad the seed of the gospel. Although sometimes local congregations lose the vision which gave them birth,[7] and doubtless, many individual Christians fall below their privileges in the Spirit-filled life, nevertheless, the New Testament Church as a whole maintains a remarkable fervency of spirit and outreach of love. Something about them makes the world aware "that they had been with Jesus" (Acts 4:13). In their lives the living Christ is lifted up, and as men see Him, revival spreads from the center to the circumference in the power of the Holy Spirit.

The Acts of the Apostles has no close. It simply breaks off the narrative by reporting that "preaching the kingdom of God, and teaching those things which concern the Lord Jesus Christ" was continuing with "all confidence . . ." (Acts 28:31). That is the way the New Testament leaves the record of revival. There is no finish. And, indeed, wherever the true Spirit of Pentecost prevails in any age, there will be no end to revival.

---

[7] Indications of this are seen in some of the letters of Paul, as for example, the condition of the Church at Corinth. The Book of Revelation also speaks of the various problems in the churches, one of which was Ephesus, a place where earlier the Christians had known real revival (Revelation 2:1–7). Pergamos, Thyatira, Sardis and Laodicea are other churches mentioned in need (Revelation 2:12–3:6, 14–22).

STUDY
ASSIGNMENTS
3

PERSONAL STUDY

1. Read the climactic account of the great post-exilic revival in Nehemiah 8:1–13:31. As you think again about the reasons for this revival, what principles do you see in the story?

What effect does obedience to God's Word have upon the worship of the people? 12:43.

According to Nehemiah 9:28, what is the pattern of revival?

2. Read the story of Jehoshaphat's reign in II Chronicles 17:1–21:1, giving particular attention to the events recorded in chapters 19 and 20. How did the king lead his people in responding to the invasion of the land by a powerful enemy?

How did the king lead his people in responding to the Word of God through the prophet Jahaziel?

What was unusual about the way the Jews went into battle?

How did the king lead his people in accepting God's victory?

Generally the twenty-five year reign of Jehoshaphat was marked by religious devotion, yet there were some evident weaknesses which led to deterioration as soon as the king died. What were they? Note II Chronicles 20:33; 20:35–37 (18:1–19:3); 21:1–6.

3. As you see it now, what is the basic problem in perpetuating revival in the Old Testament?

4. With this in mind, do you see a contrast with the pattern of revival in Jesus' ministry? If so, what is it?

5. In what sense does Pentecost form the pattern of revival in the Acts of the Apostles?

6. Reviewing your experience in the church, how would you say that the Spirit-filled life of Pentecost has dominated your congregation? Try to put your evaluation in the form of a graph. Beginning at a point on the chart representing the extent of revival twenty years ago, draw a line showing the course of revival in the years following. Of course, your evaluation is merely a broad guess, for we can never really measure the spiritual life of someone else, but still it will be interesting to look at your feeling. Let number 3 represent overflowing revival and number 0 spiritual deadness.

	20 years ago	15 years ago	10 years ago	5 years ago	now
3					
2					
1					
0					

7. Now on the same chart draw a line depicting how you see your own spiritual development during these years. As you compare the two lines, do you see any difference between your experience and that of the church in general? If one or both of the lines seems low, what are you doing to help the situation?

GROUP DISCUSSION

As you meet again in your group, center the discussion on the pattern of revival in your understanding of the Bible.* Why is there the ebb and flow all through the Old Testament? Why did Jesus take the course He did? In what sense can Pentecost be called Jesus' revival? Your answers to the personal

---

* It might be that you would like to spend more time studying the Biblical accounts of revival. If there is this interest, the references to revival noted in this chapter will point you to the most important epics.

In beginning your study, read at one sitting the whole passage. Try to get the feel of the situation. Then going back over it, ask questions which will help bring out the meaning of the text. Write down your impressions, noting any matters which you would like to explore further.

Observe the conditions showing the need for a revival. When did the events take place? What was the social and economic circumstance of the people? Were they prosperous? Poor? Depressed by others? What was the political situation in the land? Was the nation entangled in unholy alliances? Was there some great national crises which threatened the security of the country? What generally was the condition of the religious leaders? How did the people reflect the problem? Was there disregard for the law? Covenant broken? Indifference to worship and sacrifice? Ignorance of the Scriptures? Prayerlessness? Self-containment? How long had it been since the Spirit of revival was manifest on a large scale?

Once the overall problem is in view, observe how God sought to meet the need by raising up concerned leadership. Who was the human instrument through which the people were challenged? How was he qualified? Early training? Personality? Devotion to God? Knowledge of the Scriptures? How many others were faithful? Why had these men become burdened? What was the central message which God laid on their hearts? How was it presented to the people? Was a decision demanded? What gave the call a sense of urgency?

Consider then what happened in response to the challenge. Did many follow the leader? In what way? Prayer? Fasting? Confession? False altars torn down? Restitution? Scriptures studied? Obedience to the law? Sacrifices offered? House of worship restored? Was the revival progressive or sudden? In what sense? What spiritual and material benefits came to the people? Cleansing? Unity? Healing of sickness? Pro-

Bible study will open up the subject, and let the group take it from there. When you come to share your interpretation of questions 6 and 7, probably there will be some varied responses. Let each person explain his view. This will lead you to some conclusions that can direct your closing prayer.

---

tection from evil? Prosperity? How was it expressed in their feeling of gladness? Spontaneous praise to God? Singing? Generosity of gifts? What was the social good resulting from the new spirit? What effect did the revival have upon neighboring people? Was there opposition to the movement? How did it come and what was its effect? How lasting was the revival?

This last question may lead to some interesting insights concerning the decline of spiritual movements, particularly in the Old Testament. When did the revival begin to lose its vision? Why were the people frustrated in their aspirations and vows? Was repentance superficial to begin with? Did they become complacent in their blessings? Had they received adequate nurture and training in their faith? What was it? What happened to their spiritual leadership? Why were not other leaders raised up to take their place? In spite of the recoil, how was the true worship of God still kept alive?

As you analyze the course of the revival, compare it with other movements in the Bible. What did it have in common with similar awakenings? In what way did it differ? Summing up your whole study, what is the most significant lesson which you have learned from it?

Not all your questions will be answered, but following this method of inductive study will bring you to some conclusions respecting the origin and course of great revivals. Further study will gradually crystalize in your mind principles underlying these movements. Note the application of these patterns to your situation today. It is at this point that the study of Biblical revivals can have a meaningful impact on your life.

4 - A Strategy of Revival for Our Day

In the light of revival patterns in the Bible, the question might be asked: How do we relate to these guidelines today? We believe the Spirit-filled reality of Pentecost to be the norm of the Church, but when it is not, what course of action can we follow to experience revival in our time?

PERSONAL DEDICATION

Revival, like any spiritual reality, comes through personality. As E. M. Bounds puts it, "Men are God's method." [1] Programs, techniques, campaigns, and the like, are utterly useless unless the men that work the schemes are under the control of the Holy Spirit.

Full obedience is the need. God is looking for a man who will let himself go and dare to be a fool for Christ's sake. [2] Dawson Trotman put it bluntly when he said: "God can do more through one man who is 100% dedicated to Him

---

[1] E. M. Bounds, *Power Through Prayer*, (Chicago: Moody), p. 7.

[2] This was a favorite expression of Paul in describing his own commitment. He was not saying that he was uneducated, for this was not the case, but rather he was simply accepting the derision of the world as a compliment. Anytime a man identifies with the cross of Christ, both its theological content and its way of life, the world will call him a fool. See I Corinthians 1:17–4:10; II Corinthians 11:23.

than through 100 men 90% dedicated to Him." [3] Half-hearted, weak-kneed, compromising obedience will never challenge a sleeping church to rise up and rescue perishing souls from the jaws of hell. Our highly sophisticated society in the Church may look upon such unfettered zeal for Christ as fanaticism, but it is still the way that the Holy Spirit works in revival.

German pastor Pregizer of Haiterback, many years ago, once aroused his lethargic congregation by suddenly exclaiming in an Easter Monday sermon: "Fire! Fire! Fire!" "Where?" the startled congregation asked. Pregizer answered: "In disciples hearts." [4]

To be sure, that is where revival fires start—in the hearts of God's people (Hebrews 1:7). Are we combustible material? Has the promised baptism with the Spirit and with fire become a reality? Would that each of us could be as Jim Elliot when he prayed:

> God deliver me from the dread asbestos of "other things." Saturate me with the oil of the Spirit that I may be aflame. . . . Father, take my life, yea, my blood if Thou wilt, and consume it with Thine enveloping fire. I would not save it for it is not mine to save. Have it, Lord, have it all. Pour out my life as an oblation for the world. . . . Make me Thy fuel, Flame of God! [5]

LET IT BEGIN WITH YOU

Is not this the reasonable service of every Christian? Of course, it is logical to expect the church officials to lead the

[3] Dawson Trotman, quoted by Lorne Sanny in "The Adventure of a Yielded Life," *The Navigator's Log*, March–April, 1967 (Issue, 113), p. 11.

[4] Recounted by Paulus Scharpff, *op. cit.*, p. 118.

[5] Jim Elliot, taken from his journal in the book by his wife, Elisabeth Elliot, *Shadow of the Almighty* (New York: Harper, 1958), pp. 58–59, 240. Copyright © 1958 by Elisabeth Elliot. Used by permission.

way. However, the burden for revival should not rest only with these leaders, nor should it be thought essential to bring in leadership from the outside. Every member of the congregation should look upon revival as his own responsibility and find the place of service most suited to his talent and personality.

The time has come to quit thinking about the other person in the church. What about you? Regardless of what your position may be in the church, and whatever gifts you may possess, have you fulfilled the conditions for revival in your own life? Are you completely open to the Spirit's direction? Is your heart cleansed from every evil desire and selfish purpose? Mere concern for revival is not enough. Is your heart, your home, your business a witness to the overflowing love of God?

Face it! As fully as you know your will and as fully as you know the will of God, can you say that there is no competition? If not, then you are still part of the problem in the church, and before you can make a vital contribution toward its solution, you need to get in line with God's plan for your life and be filled with the Spirit of Pentecost.

Samuel Chadwick, the beloved principal of Cliff College and peer among English preachers, tells how he started his ministry infatuated with his eloquence as a speaker. Taking a pastorate in a little Lancashire cotton town, he fully expected his preaching to bring a revival to the church. But nothing happened. One Saturday night as he was going over his notes for his sermon, God revealed to him his sinful egotism. He had believed that his strength lay in his ability to preach, and he had forgotten that God alone is the source of all blessing. There was an agonizing struggle. It went on past the midnight hour. As the young preacher sought the face of God, all he could hear was: "Burn those sermons." Finally at three o'clock in the morning he kindled a fire in the kitchen grate, and the sermons were burned. As the flames consumed his elegant notes it seemed that a new fire was kindled in his heart. Revival had come, and the next day the young preacher witnessed the beginning of a mighty awakening in his church.[6]

Until such leadership is seen, there is little hope for the congregation. In some life the Church must be given an example of what revival means. Someone must show the love of God bursting forth in redemptive concern for the world; the beauty of holiness must be incarnated in human personality. People respond to a demonstration of revival, not an explanation. You be the man!

GET A COMMITTED NUCLEUS

One person burning up with the love of God invariably ignites another. It is the nature of fire not only to consume but also to spread. As the divine spark leaps from heart to heart, more and more people see the inadequacy of nominal religion, and the cry for revival is heard with increasing frequency. Gradually out of this growing concern a nucleus emerges that desires revival at any cost.

Look around for these people. Assuredly as God has dealt with you, He has spoken to others. Like yourself, they are seeking God's best. The shallow religion of our day has not deceived their spirit. They know that there are deeper riches in God's Word than have yet been fathomed, and they are open to the instruction of the Holy Spirit.

Likely such a group is waiting for direction right now in your church.[7] They may be unorganized, perhaps not even

---

[6] Told in the biography of Samuel Chadwick by Norman G. Dunning, *The Preacher as Prophet* (Athens: Georgia Bible Institute, n.d.), p. 12.

[7] In more recent history, attention might be directed to such well-known examples as the home Bible study meetings of the Pietistic revival in Germany; the Holy Club in Wesley's experience and the class meetings of the evangelical revival in England and America; the student prayer meetings at Hampden-Sydney College in Virginia and the beginning of the second awakening in America; the noon-day meetings of the great mid-nineteenth century revival; the hay-stack prayer meeting beginning the modern missionary movement; the meetings of prayer

aware of their mutual desires, but they are there, and they only need encouragement and leadership to become a dynamic force for revival. Do not worry if their numbers are few. Jesus started with just a handful, too. Any spiritual movement begins with the committed few who care. In recording history these small groups may be given little notoriety because interest naturally focuses upon the larger movements which they foster and undergird.[8] Nevertheless, the dynamic of the revival lies in these small clusters of earnest souls.

Find these concerned people who want revival. Discover what you can do together to stimulate your faith and enlarge your ministry. You do not need to break off other contacts to have this association. In fact, to give your witness an effective outlet, you must hold on to and enlarge your friendship in the church and community. But in your continuing witness through the ongoing program of the larger congregation, you dare not ignore your need to develop the potential nucleus of revival. The fallacy of so much of our church activity is that in our haste to rally the support of the crowd we neglect to cultivate the very people who ultimately must lead them.

DEVELOP A GROUP DISCIPLINE

Probably one of the most effective ways to help this nucleus grow is to meet together regularly for fellowship, prayer,

---

and confession issuing in revivals in Wales, Korea, and Africa; to mention a few. An account of some contemporary forms of this principle may be seen in Walden Howard's, *Nine Roads to Renewal* (Waco: Word, 1967).

[8] The Billy Graham Crusades are a foremost example. Though the great public meetings receive the publicity, still the real power behind a Graham crusade is generated in a whole network of small groups praying and working for the revival. Groups also play an important role in the follow-up of a crusade. Doubtless one of the greatest fruits of the Billy Graham ministry today is the organization and encouragement of small groups of earnest disciples around the world.

and Bible study. Two or three earnest souls are enough to start, though eight or nine makes a better number.

Since the group is not bound by tradition or any fixed ritual, you can work out your own discipline in the light of your particular interests. Whatever form your group might take, at its heart should be an honest determination to seek together the highest in God's purpose. In this close association of kindred spirits you can share with one another your burdens and desires. It is this family spirit which makes the small group approach so conducive to growth and gives it a depth of fellowship which the larger public services of the church cannot provide.[9]

The group must be open completely to the leadership of the Holy Spirit. Selfishness will kill it. In this willingness to let the Spirit have His way, the members must be honest with God and with each other. It may take awhile to come to this freedom and trust. After all, you are not prone to bare your soul to people that you do not know. But, as you become united in love, do not fear to be your true self. Of course, this means you must keep faith with each other and never carry beyond the group matters which are shared in confidence. The group must be careful, too, not to get off on some tangent or become complacent in its purpose. It is easy to level off on some plateau of experience and cease to

---

[9] If the function and method of group dynamics is not already understood, it would be helpful to read some of the material in this field. Among the many publications that are available for reference, particularly in the practical aspects of small groups, are: John Casteel, *Spiritual Renewal Through Personal Groups* (New York: Association Press, 1957); Harold Wiley Freer and Francis B. Hall, *Two or Three Together* (New York: Harper and Row, 1954); Robert A. Raines, *New Life in the Church* (New York: Harper and Row, 1961); Reul Howe, *The Miracle of Dialogue* (New York: Seabury Press, 1963); and Ben Johnson, *Learning to Pray* (Atlanta: Spiritual Life Publishers, 1966). For a brief yet composite picture of the whole idea, probably the best thing is the little symposium by the editors of Faith at Work entitled *Groups That Work* (Grand Rapids: Zondervan, 1967). There are also any number of smaller booklets which deal with the subject. One is the author's *Introducing the Prayer Cell* (Huntington Valley, Penna.: Christian Outreach, 1960).

press on to higher ground. Any time you lose your sense of adventure, the door of progress is closed. No matter what you have experienced thus far, there is more beyond.

A disciplined study in the deep things of God will help stretch your vision and dedication. For this reason, vital groups will need to go deep into the Holy Scriptures. There is no want of helpful material to assist in this, if needed.[10] The important thing is to keep the study exciting and personally relevant. Be creative in your methods. If one approach begins to drag, try something new. Sometimes, as a change of pace, you might want to read and discuss some provocative book or devotional classic.[11]

As you grow in the Word, so also you should grow in the experience of prayer. Where the fellowship truly pulsates with the Spirit of Christ, this should come naturally. Again you must not feel bound by old patterns of worship, but should feel free to experiment with new ways of practicing the presence of God in prayer.

---

[10] One of the best group-centered Bible studies for serious students is the program prepared by Lyman Coleman—*Growth by Groups*. It combines a vigorous discipline of personal, inductive Bible study with Scripture memorization, prayer and evangelistic outreach. The course may be ordered from Christian Outreach, Box 115, Huntington Valley, Penna. Another excellent group Bible study is available through the Billy Graham Evangelistic Association, Minneapolis, Minnesota. The basic idea of the study series is set forth in "A Guide for Leadership Training and Bible Discussion Groups."

[11] An example of a contemporary book which lends itself well to group discussion is Keith Miller's *The Taste of New Wine* (Waco: Word, 1965). A "Leader's Guide" prepared by Robert B. Doung is available to assist in group study of this book (Waco: Word, 1967). The author's, *The Master Plan of Evangelism, op. cit.,* also may be used for a group study. An instructor's guide for a leaders-in-training course using this book has been prepared by Maurice Weidman, *Christian Education and the Master Plan of Evangelism* (Wheaton, Ill.: National Sunday School Association, 1968). Examples of some devotional classics which offer rich stimulation in group study are: Francois Fenelon, *Christian Perfection* (New York: Harper and Row, 1947); Brother Lawrence, *The Practice of the Presence of God* (Mount Vernon, N. Y.: Peter Pauper Press, 1963); and Andrew Murray, *Like Christ* (New York: Grosset and Dunlap).

In your desire to draw closer to God and to love others, occasionally the group might have an overnight or weekend retreat. It is not difficult to find a place where you can get away for such a period of uninterrupted leisure, meditation and reflection. Sometimes more can be accomplished in a day on retreat than in six months of meetings in the Church.

THE OUTFLOW OF THE INFLOW

But the group dare not become occupied only with its own concerns.[12] The water of life is always flowing out to bring healing to others. Anytime that it becomes self-contained, the water stagnates and is unfit to drink. Hence as the fellowship drinks deep in the love of God there should be a growing desire to minister to others. Each person will want to find the practical way by which this can be done.

This is something which the group can discuss together, not in theoretical terms, but in down-to-earth experiences of life. In addition to encouraging personal witness in the individual sphere of influence, the group might adopt some kind of cooperative service project, such as having regular visitation throughout the community, conducting witness missions in other churches, or leading neighborhood Bible study groups designed to reach the outsider. As the members of the group give of themselves to others, the thrill of serving Christ overflows into the whole Church.

Thus the influence of the group grows. New people want to join your ranks. Other groups want to start. The experience and confidence which has been gained by the nucleus provides the reservoir of leadership for this enlarging fellowship. Periodically a group should check up on itself to see if its purpose is being fulfilled. There is no point in doing anything

---

[12] The group experience which has been described here relates basically to Christians. However, it could include anyone, provided the person is sincerely willing to seek the truth.

merely for exercise. To keep the action relevant, you may need occasionally to sharpen your discipline or perhaps change your form of meeting. The criteria for determining the value of any group always is its growth in the life and ministry of your Lord.

At times the personnel may need to divide and start new groups with different combinations of people. There is no shame in division. In fact, the division itself may be an outreach of the group, for as the group divides it forms the nucleus for other groups.

MOBILIZE THE CHURCH

With a group of dedicated people as a nucleus, the Church as a whole can be inspired and directed in the service of Christ. Of course, until this committed minority is present, there is not much use talking about getting the larger congregation involved in the task. Before there can be followers there have to be some leaders. But as the core of trained disciples grows, and the various programs of the Church are given more dynamic direction, increasing numbers of people are helped to see their own sphere of ministry.

Total mobilization of the total Church for the total ministry is the goal. Actually this is not a role peculiar to Christianity. It is a criterion of success in any enterprise involving people—be it business, government, military strategy or evangelism. All we are saying here is that the Church should be as wise in utilizing her resources as are the institutions of the world. "If our goal is the penetration of the whole world," observes Leighton Ford, "then for the agents to carry out this task we must aim at nothing less than the mobilization of the whole church." [13]

---

[13] Leighton Ford, *The Christian Persuader* (New York: Harper and Row, 1966), p. 45. Used by permission. This principle has been succinctly defined in the formula of the "evangelism-in-depth" program of The Inter-American Mission: "The growth of any movement is in direct

EVERYONE SHOULD MINISTER

The application of this principle has some revolutionary implications in the ministry of the average congregation today. For one thing, it means that everyone who participates in the life of Christ has a vital part in His ministry. Gifts and offices of individuals within His Body may differ according to God's appointment, but all of us have some unique function in the ministry of the whole Church. "A church which bottlenecks its outreach by depending upon its specialists—its pastors or evangelists—to do its witnessing, is living in violation of both the intention of its Head and the consistent pattern of the early Christians."[14]

The distinction between the clergy and the laity does not appear in the New Testament at all.[15] Moreover, the word "minister," as Elton Trueblood points out, "may be applied to anyone who ministers, regardless of the secular mode of employment."[16]

This lifts the concept of ministry into the daily life of mothers, factory workers, clerks, soldiers, farmers, students—

---

proportion to its ability to mobilize its entire membership for continuous evangelistic action." Where this principle has been applied in several united evangelistic efforts in Central and South America, unprecedented results have followed. It is gratifying to note that this concept now is being introduced in many other places around the world. An account of its beginning may be found in the book *Evangelism-in-Depth* (Chicago: Moody Press, 1961); and W. Dayton Roberts, *Revolution in Evangelism* (Chicago: Moody Press, 1967).

[14] Leighton Ford, *op. cit.*, p. 46.

[15] It is not without significance that all of the disciples called by Jesus were laymen. They were not members of the officially recognized priesthood of their day. Not until sometime after Pentecost is there any indication that members of the professional clergy joined His company (Acts 6:7). Of course, Jesus ordained some of His disciples to positions of official leadership, as did the early church, but the ordination did not set them apart for the ministry which they already shared nor did it make them a counterpart to the Old Testament priest. In the apostolic fellowship every Christian was a ministering priest before God and man.

[16] Elton Trueblood, *The Incendiary Fellowship* (New York: Harper and Row, 1967), p. 39. Used by permission.

every Christ-honoring vocation becomes a means of service and every location a place of witness.

Most of us find this concept hard to grasp. For example, as Richard Halverson observes:

> When we ask "How many ministers does your church have?" the *traditional* answer is "one" or "two" or "five," depending upon how large the paid staff is. But the *true* answer is "two hundred" or "two thousand," depending on how large the membership is! Every believer is a minister! Or when we ask, "Where is your church?" the *traditional* reply is "on the corner of Broad and Main." But the *correct* reply is "What time is it?" If it's 11:00 A.M. Sunday, then my church is "on the corner of Broad and Main." (That's where the headquarters building is!) But if it's 11:00 A.M. Tuesday, then my church is in Room 511 in the Professional Building, where Bill White, Christian attorney, is practicing law. It's at 3009 Melody Lane where Jane White, Christian housewife, is making a home. It's at Central High, where Jimmy White, Christian student, is studying to the glory of God. There is the Church in action! [17]

What a difference it would make if we would start looking at the Church ministry this way! Whatever our occupation, it would be rendered as unto the Lord. Wherever we are, it would be as in a sanctuary of worship. Every day would be filled with the glory of God. This does not mean that the secular world in which we live automatically becomes holy because we are there, but it does say that we have the opportunity within the sphere of our influence to witness in the world for Christ. It is in this sense that we are called and

---

[17] Quoted by Leighton Ford, *op. cit.*, p. 49.

sent into the ministry (John 17:18; 20:21; Matthew 28:19, 20).[18]

The church building is simply the "drill hall for the Christian task force."[19] It is the place where the soldiers come together to be trained, strengthened and briefed in the art of warfare. The battle is not fought in the Church. The battle is in the world, and church meetings are intended to prepare the church for the attack.

THE PASTOR LEADS THE TEAM

This all sounds good, but the problem comes in knowing how to relate it to our daily life. It is to help us meet this practical and constant need that the specially called pastor fulfills his function in the Body of the Church. He is the teacher ordained to train the congregation for the work of the ministry (Ephesians 4:11, 12).[20] He is not called to do all the work of the church but to help the church to do the work.

In this capacity, the pastor might be compared to a playing

---

[18] This is the basic idea in "apostolic succession." The word "apostle" means "sent ones," and it is as we go into the world with the Gospel that we truly reflect the continuity of our life with the apostle's faith and witness. There is, of course, the necessary relationships between doctrine and ministry, but merely to regard the succession as an adherence to the apostle's doctrine is not enough. Nor can the typical continuity with the apostles through the laying on of hands fulfill the intent of the matter. The succession is in the way the teachings of the apostles are carried into the world through our life, and only this kind of practical reproduction of the apostolic witness through the grace of God can keep the church from extinction.

[19] Elton Trueblood, *The Company of the Committed* (New York: Harper and Row, 1961), p. 72. Used by permission.

[20] This concept of the "equipping" ministry of the pastor has been treated by a number of contemporary churchmen. See, for example, Paul Rees, *Stir Up the Gift* (Grand Rapids: Zondervan Press, 1952); Tom Allan, *The Face of My Parish* (New York: Harper and Row, 1953); Gaines S. Dobbins, *A Ministering Church* (Nashville: Broadman Press, 1960); Thomas Mullen, *The Renewal of the Ministry* (Nashville: Abingdon Press, 1963); and Kenneth Chafin, *Help! I'm a Layman* (Waco: Word Books, 1966).

coach. It is his duty to prepare his team for the game. He knows his men, their abilities, their weaknesses, and he seeks through disciplined nurture to develop the full potential of each person. But as a playing coach, he is not a mere strategist. He plays beside his men, directing the contest from the field, not the bench. "The mark of his success is not the amount of attention which he can focus upon himself, but the redemptive character which emerges in the entire congregation or team." [21]

It can be seen that the involvement of the whole church in the ministry does not depreciate the role of the pastor. Rather, it enhances his office. By virtue of his leadership position, he is the key man in fulfilling the mission of the congregation. His pulpit is the prophetic conscience of his people, and in public and personal life, he sets the pace for others to follow.

Yet one, two, or five pastors in a church is not enough to care for the needs which are always present. The pastor will do all he can, but his strength is limited, as is yours. It must be a team effort. Only as the church enters into the ministry with him, and shares together in the joy of servant-hood, can the church fulfill her mission.

In the final analysis, the ministry is not a job; it is a life— the life of God incarnate in the flesh of His Son, and now lived by His Spirit in the Body of His Church. When this life is harnessed with the yoke of Christ, the church as a whole becomes a mighty instrument of revival.

---

[21] Elton Trueblood, *The Incendiary Fellowship, op. cit.,* p. 44.

STUDY ASSIGNMENTS
4

PERSONAL STUDY

1. Read the account of revival under the leadership of Jehoida the priest in II Chronicles 23:1–24:22. In a sentence or two, tell what you believe to be the greatest single reason for this awakening.

   Sum up in a sentence why you feel the revival ceased. Note 24:14–19.

2. As you review the revivals in the Old Testament, do you recall any great spiritual movement which did not begin in dedicated leadership, and can you think of any that continued after spiritual leadership was gone? Your answer to this question may help you appreciate more the way Jesus spent so much of His time training men to be shepherds in His church. Yet why do you suppose that Jesus developed only a comparatively small group of such men? Does this suggest anything to you about the practical requirements for dynamic teaching? Write a description of Jesus' method in developing a nucleus of revival.

3. Read carefully the account of the events leading up to Pentecost in Luke 24:49–53 and Acts 1:1–2:4. Why do you feel that Jesus insisted His disciples tarry until they be endued with power from on High?

   What were the expectant disciples doing while they waited for the promised outpouring? Note especially the following verses: Luke 24:52, 53; Acts 1:14, 24; Acts 1:16.

What strikes you about their fellowship together? Note Acts 1:14; 2:1.

4. Read the account of the day of Pentecost in *Acts 2*. How many of the disciples were involved in the witness leading up to Peter's sermon?

   When Peter gave an explanation of their witness (16–21), and then presented the claims of Christ (22–36), what effect did it have upon the people?

   Following the great harvest of converts, how did the church maintain the revival spirit? Acts 2:42–47.

5. Read Acts 3 through 6 which describes something of the continuing experience of the Jerusalem church. How did the Christians respond to persecution from without? Note Acts 4:1–33; 5:17–42; 6:9–15 (7:1–60; 12:1–25).

   How did they respond to urgent physical and social needs? Note Acts 3:1–26; 4:34–37; 5:12–16.

   How did they respond to the mounting administrative problems in the church? Acts 6:1–8.

   What was the place of the apostles in the developing structure of the church? Acts 6:4.

6. As you reflect upon the ministry of Christ multiplying through the disciples and in turn their followers, do you see this principle unfolding in your church? More specifically, do you see it in your own life?

GROUP DISCUSSION

Let your meeting this week really get at this matter of the dedicated minority leading the way for the larger congregation. Your study of revival to this point should have already focused the subject. As you talk about it together, try to come up with some plans along this line for your church. Whatever strategy you visualize, find your place in the picture. The group may then make the implementation of these plans a concern of prayer.

5 - Revival and the Mission of the Church

A practical question now needs to be raised: How do we become involved in the ministry of the Church? The usual pattern is to think in terms of looking after the Church property, working in the altar guild, helping with the every member canvass or doing some other little chore around the Church. No one will deny that these are things which need to be attended to, but is this all that our life of service involves?

That we want to do something for God is assumed, but how does a church mobilize for action.

CONTROLLING PURPOSE OF CHURCH

It is necessary again to get in mind clearly our mission as the Church. We are the Body of Christ, and as His Body on this earth, we are called to live in our body as He did in His. Evangelism thus becomes the controlling purpose in a properly functioning church body, for it was the motivating purpose in our Lord's Body—the only reason that the Eternal Son threw off the robes of glory and took upon Himself the form of our flesh. He came "not to be ministered unto, but to minister, and to give his life a ransom for many" (Matthew 20:28). Apart from His mission to save the world from sin His Body would not have been necessary.

An old lady focused the issue exactly when she turned to the guide showing her through Westminster Abbey, and said: "Young man! Young man! Will you stop your chatter for a moment and tell me—has anyone been saved here lately?"[1] Saved in Westminster Abbey? Why not? That is the business of the Church.

Any church that is discovering the thrill of revival will know this, and will be actively seeking to win the lost. Revival and evangelism, though different in nature, issue from the same source and flow together. It is true that a passion for souls is one fruit of revival, but it is also apparent that this love grows as we become involved in the work. A church which does not go out into the world to press the claims of the Kingdom would not know revival if it came.

Evangelism might be called the spiritual thermometer of the Church. When the body of believers is sick, the evangelistic program is usually the first thing to stagger. Custom and pride will keep other programs going long after their purpose is lost. Yet that part of the church activity which is not expressing the Saviour's love for lost men is simply out of touch with the Gospel. How tragic it is when the concern for fellowship, civic improvement, intellectual attainment, social welfare or some other secondary consideration, becomes the controlling passion of church life.

This confusion of priorities is doubtless one of the most bewildering problems confronting the Christian community. It is not easy to keep first things first in the Church, but it is even harder to face the consequences of not doing so. The harsh truth is that whenever evangelism is relegated to an incidental place in a church's program, the church begins to die, and unless something happens to reverse the trend, eventually the church will become extinct. The Church can

---

[1] Told by Peter Emmons, *Pattern of Things to Come*, ed. by D. McConnell (New York: Friendship Press, 1954), p. 4.

continue only as the people of God reproduce their life in each succeeding generation.[2]

This does not happen by accident. We must aim at the target to hit it. The sentimental idea that somehow evangelism will take care of itself provided we live a good life has a subtle way of beguiling us to sleep. On the other hand, a constant whirl of activity in the church is no assurance that people are being converted. Crowds may come to the Sunday services, large building programs may be completed, big budgets may be raised, tremendous energy may be expended in many worthwhile things—and evangelism may still be missing. Making Christ known and loved must become a commitment of life.

PERSONAL IMPLEMENTATION

It breaks down to a personal responsibility. No amount of programmed activity in official meetings of the church can take the place of the day-by-day vocation of personal evangelism. To assume that the formal church organization can operate on one level while the members of the body live differently is wishful thinking. The ministry of the congregation is only a reflection of the lives of individuals in the church, and this is nowhere more apparent than in evangelism.

---

[2] Evangelism is the thrust of the message of Jesus when He said that nothing could permanently prevail against His Church (Matthew 16:18). This promise followed Peter's strong affirmation of faith in Christ as the Son of the Living God (Matthew 16:16; cf., Mark 8:29; Luke 9:20). In essence Jesus said that nothing could keep His Church from reproducing as long as the Name of Christ is faithfully proclaimed. The "rock" upon which Jesus said that He would build His Church may have immediate reference to Peter's character or profession of faith, either as an individual or as a representative of all believers, but still it was the expression of this faith which caused Jesus to see His Church as unconquerable. Even so today it is the proclamation of Jesus Christ as Lord and Saviour which assures the continuation of the apostolic witness. For a discussion of this point, see the author's book, *The Master Plan of Evangelism, op. cit.,* pp. 103–105.

It is imperative that each of us make our routine contacts with other people a winsome witness for Christ. There are opportunities for lifting up Christ every day in the normal associations at home, school and work. But we must learn to speak a word for our Saviour in the right way and at the right time. Of course, this sensitivity comes through the Holy Spirit and cannot be engineered by man. But there is a sense in which we can cultivate winsomeness in our witness. One does not have to be obnoxious to be honest.

It will mean taking a genuine interest in people, listening to them, learning about their problems, showing them by our deeds that we care. When confidence has been gained, then we can explain how the Gospel which has changed our lives can also change theirs.[3]

The church might help develop these traits by providing training classes in soul-winning. This instruction should include basic knowledge of the plan of salvation, supported by at least a few Scripture verses. Every Christian needs to be able to give an unequivocal answer to anyone who wants to know the way to God.

These formal presentations will help get the idea across,

---

[3] What can and cannot be done in effective personal evangelism is painfully evident in the little book by Joseph Bayly, *The Gospel Blimp* (Grand Rapids: Zondervan, 1966). It is a walloping satire on artificial evangelism that focuses a real problem among Christians. As to the best way we can practice soul winning without being repulsively professional, each person will have to let the Holy Spirit teach him the most natural way in his situation. There are any number of books which offer helpful guidance, such as: E. Myers Harrison and Walter L. Wilson, *How to Win Souls* (Wheaton: Van Kampen, 1952); Nate Krupp, *You Can Be a Soul-Winner* (Wheaton: Lay Evangelism Crusade, 1965); Paul E. Little, *How to Give Away Your Faith* (Chicago: Intervarsity, 1966); Rosalind Rinker, *You Can Witness With Confidence* (Grand Rapids: Zondervan, 1962); Lorne Sanny, *The Art of Personal Witnessing* (Lincoln: Back to the Bible Publishers, 1957); Stephen Olford, *The Secret of Soul-Winning* (Chicago: Moody, 1963); and Charles Trumbull, *Taking Men Alive* (New York: Fleming H. Revell, 1907). Among the more effective groups today in personal evangelism, Campus Crusade for Christ deserves particular mention. Their "four spiritual laws" and other materials of evangelism may be secured from their headquarters at Arrowhead Springs, San Bernardino, California.

but a personal illustration will do much better. To really teach personal evangelism, learning disciples need to be brought into close association with those who are able to demonstrate in their lives how it is done. The church might assist in this by arranging for novices to get with those who are more experienced in witnessing.[4] This throws a heavy burden upon the few in the church who are equipped to teach, but there is no other way to do it effectively.

CHURCH PROGRAM

What is stimulated in the personal lives of the congregation, also needs to be implemented in the official program of the church week after week.[5] Soul-winning should be so fused with the structure of congregational life that if the organization functions at all, evangelism is inevitable.

The Church begins by knowing where the people are. Every person outside Christ in the area the Church serves is a special responsibility. We should learn these people

---

[4] An excellent example of this kind of training is the program developed by Reverend Jim Kennedy at the Coral Ridge Presbyterian Church in Fort Lauderdale, Florida. In this church men trained in personal evangelism are expected to train two more who in turn can train others. The program involves weekly classes at the church in conjunction with on-the-job training in home visitation evangelism. Needless to say, the church has experienced a phenomenal growth. Information about the training program including a school for interested persons may be obtained from the church office at 1901 N.E. 50 Street, Fort Lauderdale, Florida.

[5] As is the case in personal evangelism, there are many instructional materials available which show how evangelism can be brought into the various programs of the church. Most denominations will be glad to supply you with information. In addition to the official publications of your church, you might want to consult some of the following sources: C. E. Autrey, *Basic Evangelism* (Grand Rapids: Zondervan, 1959); Andrew W. Blackwood, *Evangelism in the Home Church* (New York: Abingdon-Cokesbury, 1942); J. E. Conant, *Every-Member Evangelism* (New York: Harper and Row, 1922); Bryan Green, *The Practice of Evangelism* (New York: Charles Scribner's Sons, 1951); W. E. Grendstaff, *Ways to Win* (Nashville: Broadman Press, 1957); Roland Q. Leavell, *Evangelism* (Nashville: Broadman Press, 1951); and George E. Sweazey, *Effective Evangelism* (New York: Harper and Row, 1953).

by name, know their family relationships, their social and economic needs—and this information should be followed up with definite prayer and personal concern.[6] These people are more than prospects—they are immortal souls, each one of more value in God's sight than all the wealth of the world.

Some system might be followed by which members of the church are assigned particular families to cultivate. They might be brought into neighborhood witness groups or possibly interested in a home Bible study.[7] A vigorous visitation effort also needs to be pursued by the church so that every one of these persons is lovingly confronted with the claims of the Kingdom.[8]

This compassion for the lost should be reflected in the worship services of the church. Not every service should be designed in the format of an evangelistic campaign, but the real presence of Christian love should make any sinner aware of the ever present invitation to seek God. At times, of

---

[6] The books cited in reference to general church evangelism and in visitation work will give practical help in how prospects can be found. Also, in this respect, Charles S. Mueller offers a very constructive suggestion by way of learning the geographical area of primary concern to a church and understanding community social groups in *The Strategy of Evangelism* (St. Louis: Concordia, 1965).

[7] Most of the principles discussed in reference to small groups will apply here, except that the atmosphere of a purely friendship group is more social and recreational in the beginning. In addition to the sources cited already, you might want to see Harry C. Munro, *Fellowship Evangelism Through Church Groups* (St. Louis: Bethany Press, 1951); and J. Edgar Smith, *Friendship Evangelism* (Anderson, Ind.: Warner Press, 1959).

[8] There is no lack of information in the organization and method of visitation evangelism. Each church will need to use the approach most suited to her situation. One of the most challenging of these plans is the "Salvation by Appointment" method practiced by George Delamarter and Charles Kingsley in *Go* (Grand Rapids: Zondervan, 1965). Other variations of the pattern may be seen in Shelby D. Corlett, *Soul Winning Through Visitation Evangelism* (Kansas City: Nazarene Publishing House, 1956); Horace Dean, *Visitation Evangelism Made Practical* (Grand Rapids: Zondervan, 1957); Gene Edwards, *How to Have a Soul Winning Church* (Springfield: Gospel Publishing House, 1965); Jack Hyles, *Let's Build an Evangelistic Church* (Murfreesboro, Tenn.: Sword of the Lord, 1962); and C. S. Lovett, *Visitation Made Easy* (Baldwin Park, Calif.: Personal Christianity).

course, the whole order of worship can be directed toward the outsider, leading up to a call for decision.

The same could be said of the Sunday school. Actually this is the greatest agency for evangelism in the church. For many children and youth, it is their only contact with the Gospel, and unless they are won here, they probably will not be reached at all.[9] Teachers should be prepared to deal personally with the issues of salvation in and out of the class room.

Likewise, the evangelistic concern of the church needs to be geared into the program of her auxiliary organizations, such as the Youth Fellowship, Ladies Society, Men's Club and Boy Scout Troop. These groups often attract people which are not reached through other channels of the church. Any comprehensive program of soul-winning must involve all of these special organizations. If they are not contributing to the redemptive mission of Christ, why have them in the church?

A CONTINUOUS WORK

Whatever you do, do not stop. There is no discharge in this warfare. The powers of darkness are always seeking to destroy the souls of men. To do battle with the enemy only during special seasons of the year, or merely when you feel

---

[9] There are many ways that a Sunday school can follow evangelistic programs. If you are wondering what can be done, ask your denominational headquarters to supply you with information or consult some of the many guide books which deal with this subject, such as: Edwin J. Potts, *Evangelism in the Sunday School* (Chicago: National Sunday School Association, 1960); Robert K. Bower, *Administering Christian Education* (Grand Rapids: Wm. B. Eerdmans, 1964); Kenneth Cole, *Evangelism in the Sunday Church School* (Philadelphia: Judson Press, 1955); E. P. Barrett, *A Guide for Sunday School Evangelism* (Wheaton: Evangelical Teacher Training Association, 1956); Elmer Rettner, *Evangelism in the Sunday School* (St. Louis: Concordia, 1959); Mary Latham, *Teacher You Are an Evangelist* (Kansas City: Beacon Hill, 1963); and H. W. Byrne, *Christian Education in Your Local Church* (Grand Rapids: Zondervan, 1963).

like it, is to abandon the world to the devil most of the time. If the Church is to be victorious, we must take the field with the Gospel and maintain the offensive.[10]

The Gospel is not spasmodic. By its very nature, it is always good news. So long as God is pleased to speak to dying men, the story must be told. The moment the Gospel ceases to be heard, the Church ceases to be relevant to the world.

Hence, in witness of her mission, the Church should be engaged in winning men "in season and out of season." The popular practice of a church going all-out for evangelism in some kind of annual or semi-annual event is to be commended to every congregation, but this in itself is no assurance of an adequate evangelistic concern the year around. Sometimes, in fact, these special campaigns can be used to soothe the conscience of the individual who prefers to get all of his year's work of soul-winning in ten days.

There are, of course, advantages in making special efforts to present the Gospel during periodic intervals in the church calendar, but these programs should only be an intensifying of an emphasis which is constant. There are multitudes of people who are not reached at all during these special seasons of concern. Many of them might be won if the church would practice a wise vigil for souls the year round.

BY ALL MEANS

This underscores the necessity for a variable approach. Any method which God is pleased to use in the salvation of a soul is a good method for that person. Yet each person is different, and what impresses one individual may not have

---

[10] In this connection, a very interesting summary of warfare strategy is the little book by James I. Wilson, *The Principles of War* (Annapolis, Maryland: Christian Books in Annapolis, 1964). The author, an Army officer, shows how there are certain principles of warfare which, if followed, always tend toward success in battle, but if neglected or ignored, inevitably tend toward defeat.

any appeal to another. For this reason, we must be discerning of the particular need and find methods of evangelism which are appropriate.

In His ministry, Jesus demonstrated this principle of adapting to circumstances. Practically every legitimate method used today in evangelism can be seen in some way in the work of the Master—great mass meetings, small groups, healing services, visitation campaigns, personal counseling. He could and did adjust His method to any situation. The Apostle Paul caught this spirit when he said: "I am made all things to all men, that I might by all means save some" (I Corinthians 9:22).

Of course, we should utilize to the fullest the potential of our present policy. Mention has already been made of gearing the customary programs of the church to evangelism. If these activities are meeting the need, there is no reason to change. In this connection, it might be helpful to evaluate your program in the light of its effectiveness in reaching your community with the Gospel.

When it is apparent that old methods are not getting the desired results, look around to see if there may not be better ways of doing it. We can learn from our fellow Christians in other churches. There are also many interdenominational organizations which might lift our horizons in certain areas of evangelism. When it comes to ways of communicating the Gospel, no one has a corner on the market.

Yet, sad to say, almost all of us have a tendency to get so obsessed with the two or three methods which have been particularly effective in our experience that we fail to see other, and perhaps more promising, ways of achieving our goal. Some churches act as if their survival were dependent upon a certain technique of evangelism.

While we can appreciate this nostalgia for those methods which brought us to Christ, still we must remain open to new ways the Spirit may have in reaching our generation. Of course, there is no virtue in mere newness or novelty.

Because something is new does not mean that it is any better. Closer scrutiny will reveal that the new approaches have their limitations, too. The point is that we should seek to find the best means of getting the work done. Whether or not the course of action is endorsed by long custom is entirely beside the point. The question is: Will it work?

THE VENTURING SPIRIT

This principle when followed will bring most congregations to try some different methods of evangelism. Not everything will succeed, but unless we are willing to fail in the effort, we will never find methods which will work.

It is not our purpose here to go into the myriad things which a church can do. That would take volumes, and still there would be more left unsaid. Our purpose is simply to point out the need of a church to be imaginative and creative in finding ways to fulfill her mission. There should always be an air of freshness about our approach to the hearts of men.

Do you see a place in your church where the excitement of evangelism is missing? Is it in the Sunday school? Then have you considered revising your curriculum or starting a new class designed to reach a neglected segment of your community?

Are things bogged down in the youth division? If so, have you thought of organizing a youth witnessing team or opening a Gospel Coffee House? [11]

What about your Men's Club? Do they have a vibrant ministry beyond themselves? Is the thrill of personal wit-

---

[11] Most of the coffee house experiments to date have failed to bring evangelism into their ministry, but there are some notable exceptions. For a creative approach to this concept, see Lyman Coleman, *The Coffee House Itch* (Newton, Penna.: The Halfway House, 1967). A discussion of the whole coffee house movement may be found in John D. Perry, Jr.'s *The Coffee House Ministry* (Philadelphia: John Knox Press, 1966). The Coffee Information Service at 300 East 44th Street, New York, will also be glad to supply information.

nessing evident in visitation programs? Do they ever go out and conduct open air meetings on the street? [12]

What are your young couples doing to win their friends? If they want to, but don't know how, why not talk it over next Sunday? Perhaps you could try a bowling league as a point of contact, or the ladies might take to the idea of an afternoon tea in various homes.

What are you doing to harness the media of mass communications to your evangelistic task. Have you thought about going on radio or T.V.? Could you operate a telephone service for people in distress? Does your church have a vital program of literature evangelism? [13]

Are you reaping a spiritual harvest through an effective healing ministry in the church? [14] If not, why not? Are there not people around you who need such help? The same could be said for the multiple social needs in your community, all of which offer an opportunity for the Gospel to be presented at the point where people live.

Whatever the method, the purpose is to bring evangelism into the mainstream of life. Methods are only effective as they get us involved with people. Where the ministry of Christ is brought to bear upon the felt needs of man—body,

---

[12] One of the most helpful discussions of this approach is the Manual for Salvation Army Soldiers by Lyell Rader, *Re-Discovering the Open Air Meeting* (Wilmore, Kentucky: The Department of Evangelism, 1966).

[13] A good statement in this regard is George Verwen's book *Literature Evangelism* (Chicago: Moody Press, 1963); also E. Henry Edwards and Faris D. Whitesell, *Sowing Gospel Seed* (Chicago: Moody Press, 1954).

[14] The healing of the body is vitally related to the healing of the soul. A church which ignores the ministry of healing, not only misses a great opportunity to serve human need, but also fails to realize her evangelistic potential. If some general reading in this field is desired, see Evelyn Frost, *Christian Healing* (London: Mowbrary, 1954); Bernard Martin, *The Healing Ministry in the Church* (Richmond: John Knox Press, 1960); S. I. McMillen, *None of These Diseases* (Westwood: Fleming H. Revell, 1963); Walter W. Dwyer, *Churches Handbook for Spiritual Healing* (New York: Ascension, 1965); Paul Tournier, *The Healing of Persons* (New York: Harper and Row, 1965), to suggest only a few of the many resources in this area.

mind and soul—and the approach is related to patterns of life among those we seek to reach, there will always be interest in what we have to say.

In this quest for relevance there are some exciting things going on today. Some groups are invading the public beaches to give their witness for Christ, using such means as debates, parties, films and public rallies to set up situations for personal confrontation. Some are moving into the high-rise apartment complexes to make their homes points of contact for Gospel dialogue with their neighbors. Some are using breakfasts and luncheons to get together professional people for fellowship, prayer and study of the Word. Some are going deep into gambling dens and red light districts to start street missions and counseling services. Some Christian athletes are using their popularity to reach young people in football clinics, concluding with an evangelistic rally in the high-school auditorium. Some are using youth rehabilitation programs and Christian camps to reach delinquents in the slums of our cities.

The list could go on and on. There is no end to what can be done to introduce people to Christ. As to what methods are best in your situation, who can say? But whatever is done, whether it be something new or old, if it is to mean anything, it must issue from the pure motive of love to God.

THE PRINCIPLE IN LIFE

Indicative of this spirit is the work of Bill Iverson in Newark, New Jersey. Frustrated in his efforts to reach the people around his large downtown church, he decided to buy a restaurant across the street from the local high school and seek to establish contact with young people while serving them light snacks. Soon he began to penetrate the life of the community, and before long some of the youth were converted.

Using a survey to open up the conversation, Mr. Iverson

sought to draw out the spiritual feelings of the youth. As dialogue developed, reinforced within the context of mutual respect, the young person often became interested in the Christian faith. This led to a positive sharing of what Christ means. Contacts were followed up through visitation in the home, and those wanting to learn more about the Christian life were brought into "Encounter Groups." In these little fellowship cells they matured in the faith and eventually were channeled into some kind of meaningful witness.

It was tough going at first. There were few who seemed to share Bill Iverson's vision. After several months the financial burden was more than he could swing, and he had to close up. As he shut the door and walked down the street, the cop on the corner said with tears in his eyes: "I hate to see you leave, Bill. This is the greatest thing that's ever happened on this block."

When the doors closed, some of the recently won teenagers came to Bill and offered to work without pay to keep the restaurant open. Others volunteered support, and with their help, hamburgers and the Gospel soon started again to move across the counter.

Bill's Rough Riders Luncheonette, named after the high-school football team, may still be having difficulties making ends meet, but it is probably reaching more unreached young people with the claims of Christ than any other ministry in the city. The work now includes a Street Academy for school dropouts; occasional luncheonette parties; youth retreats; athletic teams; meetings in high schools; personal work with addicts, runaways and wards of the court; along with various ministries to church groups.

The alertness of these people to opportunity is reflected in their immediate response to the Newark riots in 1967. When the city erupted in bloody fighting, Bill Iverson and his associates were right in the middle of it offering coffee and the care of Christ to National Guardsmen and black men alike. During the height of the conflict, the little restaurant remained open day and night as a center of healing to distraught souls. Today, as in that time of crisis, it stands as a symbol of the way Christ is ever seeking to communicate His love to a lost world.

There is nothing pretentious or spectacular about it. All they are trying to do is "to meet youth where they are, as they are, for what they yet shall be." Their method is simply "to be available to Jesus Christ to be Himself in us, twenty-four hours a day, one day at a time." [15]

When all is said and done, is not this all that any of us can do? In the final analysis, methodology has to be incarnated in a person, a person fully "available to Jesus Christ."

Here is precisely where revival and evangelism become one—the point where love turns into action. Where such love abounds, ways will be found to get out the Gospel, whatever it takes.

---

[15] Taken from a Cross Counter news letter, Easter, 1967. A brief story of this ministry is told in *Faith at Work*, May–June, 1965, and *Guideposts*, February, 1967. Further information may be obtained from Cross Counter, Box 6045, Newark, New Jersey.

STUDY ASSIGNMENTS
5

PERSONAL STUDY

1. Looking again at Luke 24:48, 49 and Acts 1:8, why do you think that the outpouring of the Holy Spirit is linked with witnessing?

2. This raises the question, what is meant by evangelism? Is it merely a spoken testimony, or does it involve the presentation of Christ through the total witness of our life? Write out a definition of evangelism as you understand it.

3. With your definition in mind, paraphrase Acts 1:8.

4. You have already considered how this commission was carried out in Jerusalem and the environs of Judea (Acts 2–7). Now note how the witness of Christ penetrated to regions beyond. Read the account of revival at Samaria in Acts 8:1–25. Who first carried the Gospel to Samaria, and what served to get them out? 8:1–4

   How did Philip minister in word and deed? 8:5–7

   What effect did his ministry have upon the Samaritans? 8:8–13

   Why did the apostles send Peter and John to Samaria?

5. Read carefully the account of Philip leading the Ethiopian to Christ in Acts 8:28–40. List at least four basic principles of personal evangelism which you see in this story.

6. Acts 10:1 through 11:18 tells how the Gospel came to the Gentile house of Cornelius. Why do you suppose that the

breakthrough of the Gospel to the non-Jewish world began with a little group of devout people already seeking God? Note 10:1–5, 30–33.

7. From here follow the outreach of the Gospel into the Gentile world in Acts 11:19–30 and 13:1–4. Again who were the ministers of Christ bearing the good news to these places?

How did the Jerusalem church help encourage and give direction to this new advance?

How did the Antioch church respond to the physical needs of their brethren in Judea?

When this growing church at Antioch realized the missionary call of the Spirit, how did they react? Acts 13:1–4 (14:25–28; 15:30–35; 18:22–23)

Why do you think this church sensed so keenly their evangelistic responsibility to the world? Sum up your thoughts in a sentence or two.

8. Looking at your church, how is your spiritual life finding expression in your evangelistic work at home and abroad? To help focus the matter, perhaps it would be well to make a mental note of the number of new people in your community who have been won to Christ through your witness this past year. In terms of your world vision, how many have gone to the mission field from your church and how many missionaries do you now fully support? And what about the social needs of your community? Are you truly involved in the heartbreak of those around you?

GROUP DISCUSSION

In your group this week, come to grips with the work of the Holy Spirit in evangelism. Let each person share his view in this respect. Then discuss what you are doing about it. It might be well to list all the various ways now that your church is seeking to reach men. What are your most effective methods? Where is there need for improvement? In the light of question 8, are you satisfied? Here is a good place to center your prayers.

6 - Planning a Revival Meeting

We come at last to consider the planning of church revival meetings. You may wonder why we have taken so long to introduce this subject. But the reason has already been implied. It is necessary to see these special services within the context of the total church mission and strategy. If this emphasis is isolated from the constant program of the church, as if we can have revival only at particular times or through certain methods, then we have missed the whole meaning of revival. Obviously a series of meetings is not enough. Still, where the services bring into focus the meaning of vital Christian experience, and create a situation for people to seek God in earnest, there is no reason why a revival meeting cannot live up to its name.

KEEP THE PURPOSE CLEAR

Remember that our first concern is to awaken the church to her potential power. ". . . judgment must begin at the house of God . . ." (I Peter 4:17), which is another way of saying that the saints must move up if the sinners are to move in. There is no place for superficiality in program or message. If the revival is to reach far it must go deep. Any compromise with this principle for momentary appeal will be self-defeating.

Implementing this concern will mean that the great holiness themes of Scripture need to be given preeminence in the meetings. Simple Bible exposition is the need with an emphasis upon daily living of the victorious Christian faith. We must get down to the practical disciplines of life, giving attention to such needs as daily worship, family religion, personal ethics, social obligations and witnessing in our work.

Of course, the evangelistic challenge to the outsider cannot be neglected. Unbelievers brought within the sphere of the meetings should understand what they must do to be saved and be given opportunity to express their need. But the primary burden of a revival meeting is to get the church to be the church. A church revival then becomes a launching pad for all-out evangelism.

PREPARATION IS THE KEY

Meetings for this purpose may come about in many ways. In some cases they are a traditional part of the annual church calendar. In other instances they may be scheduled in cooperation with a larger District or Conference program. Sometimes a congregation just decides to have a meeting because the time seems right.

In any event, a revival meeting, like any other effective church program, is going to require the full exercise of every talent that God has given. It involves painstaking planning. God may very well overrule our plans and send revival in a way which we have not expected—an option always welcome when God chooses to exercise it.[1] Even so, this possibility does not excuse us from doing everything we can

---

[1] When revival really comes to a whole congregation, we need not worry about methodology in a meeting. The Spirit of God will take care of the situation Himself and any method then will work. But where a church has only a small segment who are in the full sway of the Spirit, as is the case in most situations, utmost care must be exercised in seeking to involve larger numbers in the meeting.

to prepare the way of the Lord. What happens during the meeting usually reflects the vision and dedication which have gone into it. In fact, most of the real work is done before the formal meetings begin.

This underscores again the need for a growing nucleus of disciples in the Church who are willing to let God have His way in their lives. As this group gives leadership to others, and more of the congregation become involved in the ministry of the Church, a strong working force for revival is assured. These people, strategically placed in positions of influence, put the needed get-up-and-go in the effort. Without them, the meeting will flounder for lack of leadership.

GEAR TO YOUR SITUATION

Local conditions will determine largely the particular structure of the meeting. Since every situation is different, adjustments will have to be made in almost any scheme proposed by this or any other general church manual.[2] Common sense is probably our best policy at this point.

Look at the situation from every angle. Consider what has been tried in the past and how it has succeeded. Weigh carefully the working schedules of your people, their patterns of leisure, their attitudes toward various methods of evangelism. What type of program would appeal most to their interests? When is the best time to have a meeting? How long should it last? Where would be the best place to conduct services?

---

[2] In addition to books already cited in church evangelism, helpful counsel in preparing for church meetings may be found in C. E. Matthews, *A Church Revival* (Nashville: Broadman Press, 1955); Charles H. Morris, *Preparation and Promotion of a Revival* (Grand Rapids: Zondervan Press, 1956); George Sweeting, *The Evangelistic Campaign* (Chicago: Moody Press, 1955); and John R. Bisagno, *The Power of Positive Evangelism* (Nashville: Broadman Press, 1968). Denominational headquarters also will have helpful material to assist local congregations in preparing for crusades. The same holds true for most evangelists who are constantly engaged in this type of ministry.

51510

Will special workers be invited to assist in the effort? [3] How can the revival emphasis be extended into the community? What will be a realistic budget and how will it be raised? What will be done to follow up those who make decisions? How does the church plan to continue the revival concern? These and other questions should be considered objectively in the early period of planning.

DEVELOP A PLAN

Most meetings will follow a general spiritual life and evangelistic theme. However, sometimes you may want to give the message a special focus. For example, it might center on prayer, missions or Bible prophecy. Possibly the services could follow the pattern of a youth crusade, family life conference, Sunday school revival [4] or Lay Witness Mission.[5]

---

[3] God has given some people in the church the special office of evangelist (Ephesians 4:11; Acts 21:8; II Timothy 4:5). This does not imply that others are not called to evangelize, but rather it emphasizes the particular leadership function of this gifted person in the ministry of the whole Body of Christ. The Church should avail herself of these persons who have this obvious ability. However, it would be well to check thoroughly into the previous ministry of such persons before one is called to lead in your situation. Like everything else about the human equation, evangelists have different talents and temperaments, and the church should understand these differences in deciding upon the persons most suited to their need. There are times, too, when a pastor might be the first choice to lead a given meeting.

[4] In this kind of meeting the Sunday school meets usually for forty-five minutes before or after the regular preaching service each evening. Where classes meet before the rally, instruction may be given in the subject later to be expounded by the pastor. Where classes meet after the rally, they can provide a means for discussing the sermon or having a follow-up Bible study. Usually on the final night there is a dedication service. If desired, a teacher training class may be scheduled during the day.

[5] A Lay Witness approach centers in personal testimony by dynamic Christian laymen who come to share their experiences. The public meetings may be supplemented by fellowship dinners, prayer breakfasts, discussion groups and personal visitation. For more information about this form of revival, see Ben Johnson's book, *Road to Renewal* (Atlanta: Spiritual Life Publishers, 1966). Also, note the book by Claxton Monro and W. S. Taegel, *Witnessing Laymen Make Living Churches* (Waco: Word, 1968).

101

A well-balanced program should include various ministries of outreach during the day. There might be early prayer services, groups meeting at breakfast or lunch, morning study periods, afternoon visitation or training sessions, evening youth groups, and any number of other activities scheduled to supplement the featured night rallies.[6] On rare occasions you might even want to arrange a continuous series of services in the church for a sustained period of time.[7]

The church building may be the focal point of activity, but do not restrict services to this central meeting place. Something should be done to get the revival out into the places where people live. Meetings of various kinds can be arranged in homes, schools, factories, business houses, hotels, restaurants, jails, hospitals, theaters and on the streets. The medium of mass communication can be used to carry the revival message still farther out into the community.

Leave no stone unturned in working out the details of your plan. Be imaginative! During the time of scheduled meetings an effort should be made literally to saturate the area with the witness of revival. The more different ways that you can involve people in the effort, the better it will be. The only limitation to what can be done is the personnel you have available to direct the programs.

SET A SCHEDULE

Once the general guidelines of policy have been determined, dates need to be set and the church calendar cleared

---

[6] Visiting workers can handle some of these meetings, but the pastor and other church leaders will need to carry their load. Where an invited evangelist is expected to lead these services, it is a good policy to clear with him first.

[7] When this is done, usually the services are scheduled to last through a period of twelve to twenty-four hours. During this time preaching periods may be interspersed with singing, testimonies, prayer, discussion groups, films, training classes, debates, etc. The idea is to have something going on all the time on a scheduled basis, with people free to come and go as they wish. A prayer vigil can continue the meeting through the night.

of any competing program during the revival meeting. It would be well also to check with other community activities to avoid conflicts of interest as far as possible. Where special workers are to be invited to assist in the meetings, it may be necessary to make arrangements long in advance.

The actual organizing of a meeting should begin to take shape about four months prior to the event. By this time committees should be delegated and beginning to function. Three months before the scheduled meetings, things should be well under way, with the pace accelerating as the time of the meeting draws near.

DELEGATE AUTHORITY

Thorough preparation necessarily requires organization. No amount of spiritual dedication is a substitute for this tedious work. To leave the preparation of a revival meeting to impulse is to discredit the intelligence which God has given to His people. Organization alone is no sign of Christian commitment, but on the other hand, God is not the author of confusion.

The official responsibility for planning the meeting usually rests with a commission amenable to the official board. This group normally is composed of duly authorized representatives from every department of the church. The pastor, as a member of the group, naturally will have a lot to say about any revival plans, but responsibility for setting up and directing the meeting rests with the whole body. Sometimes these committees of the church may seem cumbersome, and unnecessarily slow, but if we are to expect total church participation in the effort, we will have to work through the established channels.

Through this special group, the revival plan is interpreted to the whole congregation in terms of what each person is expected to do. Everyone in some way should be enlisted in the effort. Work responsibilities must be spelled out in detail by the commission and then assigned to specific people.

Usually these areas of responsibility are delegated to committees of one or more persons, depending upon the size of the church. Where existing committees already have jurisdiction in a given area, such as visitation or music, work in that area can be given to them. In areas where the church has no group presently working, special committees can be set up for the revival meeting. It does not matter so much about the structure of these working groups. All that matters is that they be able to handle the work assigned to them, and that they will be willing to do it.

AREAS TO BE COVERED

The following areas of responsibility embrace the general set-up for a local church meeting. Not everything suggested in any category can be carried out in a revival effort, but something in each area should be done. As you go through these areas, note what applies in your case.

1) *Prayer.* Revival comes through prayer. To overlook this in planning a meeting would be tragic indeed. So in addition to intensifying the regular intercessory ministry of the church, it would be well to undergird the revival with some special programs of prayer. For example, home prayer meetings can be scheduled in various homes and business places, preceding and continuing through the meeting.[8] Prayer times can also be arranged around breakfasts and

---

[8] These informal prayer meetings can be conducted in different sections of the community and at different times during the day and night. The groups may meet every day or only once or twice a week, depending upon the situation. Announce the schedule in all church media. Invite the people to attend the meetings best suited to their schedule and locality. Each group should have a host and a prayer leader. The host sees that everything is ready for the meeting and welcomes the people as they arrive. The leader is responsible for conducting the services. Always start and end on time. See that everyone is acquainted. The service may consist of a brief Bible reading, testimonies, sharing of requests, and a general session of prayer in which everyone is invited to participate. The whole meeting usually lasts between thirty minutes and one hour.

luncheons in hotels and restaurants. Taking an idea from Pentecost, prayer services might be scheduled for ten days at the church before the meeting. A prayer vigil might be set for twenty-four hours sometime in connection with the revival. Pre-service prayer meetings can be announced. The congregation could be asked to pause for a moment of prayer at a given time each day. Prayer lists can be circulated to shut-ins. Reminders to pray can be placed in hymnals, telephones and in all church mailings. Prayer requests can be sent to other churches. To help sharpen the spiritual vision for revival, a prayer retreat might be scheduled for all committee chairmen and church leaders sometime before the meeting. If desired, a dedication service could be arranged at the church for all the revival workers the day before the formal meeting starts.

2) *Prospects*. The church should always have an up-to-date list of people for whom particular prayer is being offered and continuous concern manifested. If this is not the case in your church, something will have to be done about it to focus the outreach of the meeting.

3) *Visitation*. We must go after people to win them. This continuing responsibility of the church should be strengthened by the revival. Some visitation may be simply to make friends and invite them to the services. Other callers can visit prepared people with the idea of presenting the claims of Christ and asking for a decision. These assignments are made from the prospect list. Usually the visitors meet in the evening for briefing and prayer, perhaps following a light meal. They are paired in teams and sent out to call in assigned homes. After the calls are completed, they return and report the result. If this is not already a part of the church program, it certainly needs to be instituted for the revival. In connection with the visitation, interviews might be arranged for the evangelist and pastor to visit with city officials and leading public figures.

4) *Lay Witness.* There is no revival in the church without joyous Christian testimony nor is there anything more convincing to the skeptical world. This witness should be reflected in the public services and also given expression in the small groups. Those groups already meeting can enlarge their outreach by inviting new friends in for fellowship and Bible study. Attention might be given to starting some new groups oriented to the interest levels of particular professions, such as doctors, school teachers or foreign students. In other areas, teas might be arranged for women in the afternoon, during which time some dynamic lady can share her Christian experience. Also, following the services each night, people might be invited to various homes for an after-glow discussion. If help is needed, laymen from other churches will be glad to come in and share their witness in the services. Arrangements can be made for these visiting laymen to stay with the people.

5) *Sunday school.* Since this is the greatest agency for evangelism, it would be virtually impossible to have much of a revival without bringing the Sunday school into it. Enlist every teacher in the effort. Classes can assist in promoting attendance. Perhaps the revival meeting could work in with a Record Attendance drive,[9] or Decision Day [10] emphasis in the Sunday school.

---

[9] A record goal of attendance is set for the Sunday school and broken down by departments and classes. Teachers are asked to contact every pupil and urge their attendance. On the appointed day when the roll has been taken in the classes, the Sunday school, from the Junior Department up, goes into the church sanctuary. After a few songs, the evangelist is introduced and his message takes the place of the lesson. He presents the plan of salvation and gives an invitation. The service may go on into the regular church hour or dismiss in time for morning worship.

[10] A Decision Day follows much the same pattern as the Record Attendance Day, except that it is aimed only at the Juniors, Intermediates and Youth, and it does not necessarily involve any attendance campaign. However, it should be preceded by the teacher's personal counsel with pupils who are not clear in their experience with Christ. The Decision Day approach is not recommended unless this pre-service visit, preferably in the home, is completed.

6) *Children.* Something special should be done to make children aware of their place in the Kingdom. Perhaps children's services could be arranged in the afternoon or preceding the evening rally. It might be possible to announce the meetings through the grade school, or even better, have a service at the school. Of course, good leadership is essential, which may involve securing the help of some gifted children's worker.

7) *Youth.* Here is where the action usually starts. Young people want to be challenged, and when you get their attention, revival makes sense. Seek the cooperation of the high-school teachers and coaches. If possible, arrange a service in the school. Get names of all students and send them a personal letter inviting them to the revival meeting. Contact all youth organizations in the community, such as the Boy Scouts, Girl Scouts, 4-H Clubs, Hi Y; extend invitations to attend the service as a group. Work with college organizations in getting to the students. Involve young people in your visitation efforts. Arrange some functions especially for the youth, like a breakfast each morning or a banquet on Saturday night before the public service. An open discussion might be arranged for the college set. Talkback sessions after the evening services usually meet with approval, too.

8) *Music.* Revival sets people to singing. To provide direction to this joyful impulse, a great musical program each evening should be arranged. Secure a good song leader. See that a choir is present each night. Existing choirs of the church can be used, or a special group can be formed for the meetings. Trained accompanists will need to be ready. Sometimes a band or orchestra can be assembled. Make sure sufficient song books are available. Select a theme song for the meeting, singing it each night to open or close the services.

9) *Nursery.* To encourage young adults to attend, arrangements should be made to care for their small children during the meetings. The best way is to have a nursery staffed with competent attendants. If your church does not

have such facilities, then a nursery should be set up in a home. You may also compile a list of trustworthy baby sitters who would be glad to go to the house of young parents and stay with their children for a reasonable fee.

10) *Attendance.* Though most of the areas of responsibility involve attendance, there are some things along this line that will require attention. For example, you could promote a fill-a-pew plan several nights. This is a system whereby each pew in the church is assigned to a captain who is expected to fill the seats by inviting friends to the services. Another way to stimulate interest is to designate a particular group for recognition each night, such as the official board, ladies society, young couples, etc. Probably one of the most productive methods of encouraging attendance is to invite guest delegations to the services. The invitations should be extended personally to every church, civic club, industry and business in the community. It must be done well in advance and assurance must be given that seats will be reserved so each group may sit together as a body. In some places it will be necessary to arrange transportation for those wanting to attend the meetings.

11) *Publicity.* Let the community know that you want revival. Several months before the meetings, start submitting news stories to local newspapers. Try to get off of the religious page and into the news section. It will be worthwhile to place an eye-catching ad in the paper on the day the meeting begins, and continue a small notice throughout the meeting. Give announcements to all radio and TV stations which report local news. Posters may be put in prominent places around town. Ask your people to place bumper stickers on their cars, and also give them a plentiful supply of cards and leaflets to send to their friends. The young people could distribute throughout the community printed folders describing the meeting. Flyers can be made available to food stores to pack with groceries. A large sign might be put up in front of the church, and if possible, a streamer across the highway.

Have some of the ladies, using a crisscross telephone directory, call every number within a mile of the church and invite the people to the meetings. Spot announcements can be arranged on local radio and TV stations.

12) *Facilities.* The place of public meeting should be ready for worship. See that the building is clean, hymnbooks neatly arranged, floors swept, etc. Also, take care of the lighting, temperature, ventilation. Be sure that the public address system is checked out well in advance each night. Sometimes it may be necessary to make special arrangements for the after service. If necessary, provide extra seats and any other equipment needed in the service.

13) *Ushers.* Those who come to the services should be made to feel at home. Greeters stationed at each entrance before and after the services can help create this atmosphere of friendliness. Of course, a sufficient number of ushers should be present to assist in seating people and receiving the offering. They should also be prepared to handle any disturbances which may occur. Parking attendants may be outside to help direct traffic.

14) *Hospitality.* A worker is worthy of his hire. Arrangements will need to be made to care for the visiting workers' lodging, food, and possibly, transportation. It might also be nice to plan a reception for them some night after the service.

15) *Finance.* Any well prepared program today costs money—a lot more than most churches realize. What this will be and how the amount will be raised is something which should be agreed on well in advance.[11] Those responsible for carrying out these policies should prepare a tentative budget

---

[11] Where special workers are invited to help in the services, financial obligations should be frankly discussed at the time arrangements are made. Men who are engaged full time in this itinerant ministry will be glad to discuss their policy with church leaders. Evangelists and their families usually are supported entirely by the remuneration given to them in these meetings. They deserve a fair compensation for their labors.

in consultation with church leaders, they should receive and deposit all offerings, solicit special contributions, pay all bills, and submit to the church board an audited report after the meeting is over.

16) *Follow-up.* The enduring value of the revival is determined largely by the direction given those who make commitments. Usually those who have this responsibility will need some special training in procedures to be followed. The nature of this kind of work will be discussed in the next lesson.

THERE ARE NO SHORT-CUTS

The responsibilities which have been briefly outlined here are basic to any general church meeting. As has already been emphasized, it will be necessary to adjust committees and plans to each situation, but everything should be done to make the revival services truly dynamic.

Where adequate preparation is not made, merely having a series of public meetings is not recommended. For this reason most so-called "revival meetings" should never be conducted. Rather than stumbling half-heartedly through the forms of another meeting, it would be best to go to work in laying the foundation for a real revival, looking toward full-scale public meetings when the church is ready.

A revival crusade demands sacrifices. It means hard work. It will take time and money. There will be innumerable difficulties to overcome, any one of which could be defeating. To see your plans come true, there must be methodical, painstaking, undaunted determination to have revival at any cost.

Where this is your intent, and you are willing to commit your total resources to its fulfillment, the crusade should be both the consummation and the renewal of the church revival effort.

STUDY ASSIGNMENTS

6

PERSONAL STUDY

1. Read the account of the revival at Ephesus in Acts 18:18–20:1. How did the work get started?

When Apollos came to town and began to preach in the synagogue, what limited the spiritual effectiveness of his ministry?

Apparently the eloquent Apollos received more understanding of the Gospel through the witness of Aquila and Priscilla (18:26–28), but what effect did his early ministry have upon those who followed his teaching?

When Paul again came to Ephesus and learned about these men, who only knew the message of John the Baptist, how did he deal with the problem?

With this little group now awakened by the Spirit, Paul proceeded to gather the spiritually sensitive out of the synagogue (19:8). When opposition came to his ministry, they withdrew to a private home where Paul continued to instruct the learners in the way of Jesus (19:9). Many miraculous works of charity also were done by Paul (19:11, 12). But most significantly, within the next two years all of the inhabitants of that province in Asia heard the Gospel of Christ. How did it happen? Note Acts 19:10 (19:26).

Note some other evidences of real revival in this church. Note Acts 19:13–20.

2. As you think about the development of this revival, beginning with a dedicated couple, then going to a small band, then to a larger group out of the synagogue, and finally to the multitudes of the area, how does this reflect upon the pattern of revival seen elsewhere?

3. Reflecting upon the methods employed in connection with the work at Ephesus, list some of the different ways that Paul ministered. Note the following references: 18:18; 19:1, 2; 19:5; 19:8; 20:1; 20:4.

4. Paul's statement in I Corinthians 9:22 sums up this idea. Put this verse in your own words.

5. In thinking about a revival meeting as one way of reaching people, how do you see this method making a real contribution to your continuing evangelistic ministry?

6. What do you conceive to be the primary goal of this kind of effort? Is it aimed at the church or the world? Explain what you mean.

7. In implementing your objective, how extensive should be the program of such a meeting? With this in mind, note some things that can be done to make the meeting more effective. Be specific.

8. What part in the revival preparation are you willing to assume?

GROUP DISCUSSION

Your group today should get at the purpose for a revival meeting, or for that matter, any kind of spiritual life emphasis. Zero in on your objectives and from this consider your methods. Discuss your experiences along this line in other years. Then work out some realistic plans for your situation now. These guidelines for action may give content to your prayers.

7 - Continuing the Revival Spirit

Revival should be continuous. As a method of stimulating concern, special crusades have their limits, but the spiritual reality of revival is not dependent upon big meetings to keep it going. However, the question must be asked: How is the spirit of revival maintained?

RECOGNIZE THE PROBLEM

There is no point in denying that, too often, there is a tendency to let down after the formal crusade is over. Some of this may be due to emotional exhaustion and may be only a necessary release from the tension that follows a sustained period of concentration. But this is not what we are talking about. The problem that we refer to is one of spiritual decline, and it reflects upon the genuineness of the revival itself.

Naturally those who were swept into the revival current merely on the wave of emotional sentimentality will soon fall away. Since they live more by feeling than by faith, when the enthusiasm of the meeting subsides they have nothing to hold on to. Such people can be salvaged, but they will need to be brought to a true Christian commitment anchored in the Word of God.

There are others who have made a sincere decision to follow Christ, yet who are so immature in their faith that they

114

are easily discouraged and overwhelmed by temptation. Where these new Christians are not established in the meaning of their experience, as so often happens, it is easy to understand why so many young converts fall away.

But probably even more frustrating to the effect of revival is the way that some older Christians fail to bear fruit after the meeting is over. It is not that they cease to identify with the church, but that they lose their zeal to see the revival spread and deepen. After a while they become content to coast along in the same old patterns as before. Mediocrity sets in. Some who were prominent in the meeting become casual in their responsibility to the church. The blessings of revival are appreciated, and the remembrance of former days may be venerated, but there is no real effort to perpetuate the dedication which called them forth.

RETREAT BRINGS DEFEAT

What we may fail to comprehend is that the fruits of revival can endure only as the conditions for revival are maintained. There must be continual openness to the Spirit's direction. As He leads on to deeper truths in Christ, we must follow. Where we see a wrong deed or attitude in our life, obedience to Christ demands that we confess our sin, forsake it, and by faith in the covenant of grace renew our dedication. And, as we grow in grace and knowledge—continuing in prayer and thanksgiving—our Christian witness should find expression in deeds of love.

Complacency invariably undermines revival. When the spirit of sacrifice wanes, people become self-conscious, and this disposition leads to criticism and dissension within the church. Minor concerns come to the fore and, before long, good people get so involved in their own little pursuits that they have no time for soul-winning.

As the Christian community withdraws within itself, the Church is pressed to think in terms of self-preservation.

Energy is diverted from attack to defense. Daring faith, which before had swept everything in its wake, now becomes halting and conciliatory. Things may go along all right for awhile, but the thrill of victory is gone. Revival loses its radiance. It does not die; it just fades away—the life gradually leaks out of it—the vision vanishes.

There are some who seek to keep alive something of the revival witness. Unfortunately, however, these stalwart disciples often become withdrawn from the leadership of the Church. They are a stabilizing influence, and have a very wholesome ministry, but even they may fail to reproduce their life and vision in others.

FOLLOW-UP OF NEW CHRISTIANS

Thorough follow-up is the place to begin. The Church must provide incentive and leadership to those who have resolved to obey Christ. Without it the revival has no enduring value. We dare not get so thrilled with the rescue of the perishing that we leave these sheep already gathered to the prey of wolves.

New Christians are especially in need of personal care.[1] They are but "babes" in their new life in Christ (I Peter 2:2), and, like any infant child, must have spiritual guardians to feed them, protect them, and guide them if they are to survive. This can only be done by fellow Christians who have Shepherd's hearts. Materials and programs, excellent as they

---

[1] An excellent treatment of the whole subject of follow-up is Waylon B. Moore's volume, *New Testament Follow-up for Pastors and Laymen* (Grand Rapids: Wm. B. Eerdmans, 1963). Other helpful books are those by Arthur C. Archibald, *Establishing the Converts* (Philadelphia: Judson Press, 1952); and Sidney Powell, *Where Are the Converts?* (Nashville: Broadman Press, 1958). Above all, read Dawson Trotman's, *Born to Reproduce* (Lincoln, Nebraska: Back to the Bible, 1957). The founder of The Navigators sums up in this straightforward message the most sensible method of winning and training men to reproduce the Gospel.

may be, are no substitute for loving, personal attention. True spiritual concern must be demonstrated by persons directly associated with those they are seeking to help.

With this in mind, the Church will need some kind of system to assure that each new disciple has a Christian-fellowship friend. This is a matter too crucial to leave entirely to individual impression. It might be that a special committee will need to be set up to direct this program.[2] Its responsibility would be to assign counselors to young converts and to receive regular progress reports from the counselors. If a less formal structure of organization is desired, perhaps the follow-up could be supervised by one of the growth groups in the church.

Regardless of the way the program is structured, it will involve a lot of people, and the number needed will increase as the revival harvest grows. Needless to say, such personal work does not come by wishful thinking. People for this work must be enlisted and trained. Again, the little nucleus of committed Christians around which the revival emerged will be most sensitive to this situation, and they will need to lead the way for others.

IMMEDIATE HELP

Follow-up of new Christians, like any pediatric care, should begin at birth. For this reason, in public services it is well to have trained counselors ready to assist those who have re-

---

[2] This is usually called an "Adoption" or "Sponsor" plan. The way such a committee is set up would depend upon the local church structure. The pastor or a leading layman could be its chairman. Personnel on the committee should be representative of the church, with special attention given to the Youth Department. It might function as a part of a larger body, such as the Commission on Evangelism or even the Church Board. Normally it would want to meet at least monthly, though its function should be immediate as the need arises. For a good treatment of the organization and work of this committee, see Waylon B. Moore, *op. cit.,* pp. 80–106.

sponded to the invitation. Normally, they should be of the same sex, and near the same age, except when dealing with children or members of the family. It is customary for the counselor to go forward and take a position next to the seeker or to stand by and wait for assignment by the pastor. If the meeting takes place at an altar, the counselor may want to come to the inside of the communion rail. In the case of an inquiry room, the counselor may take a place in a chair next to the seeker.

The seeker should be allowed to pray without interruption as long as he wants. When it is time to speak, the counselor can introduce himself and, by asking questions, help the person to clarify what has happened.[3] The assumption is that the seeker has something to settle, either by way of confirming a decision made earlier or to make a new com-

---

[3] For example, a question might be asked: "Jim, why did you come forward tonight?" The idea is to get the person to state the reason for his coming. If he does not know, as sometimes happens, then the counselor may help him locate the problem by asking probing questions, such as: "Jim, did you sense an uncertainty about your salvation?" Until there is assurance that the need is met, the seeker is not ready to go, although he may want to be left alone to pray. Lack of assurance may be caused by four things. (1) It may be due to a misunderstanding of the promise. Some people have the mistaken idea that an assurance of salvation is the privilege only of a few especially pious people. In this case it would be well to ponder I John 5:11–13 and, as a follow-up, to read through the whole letter of I John, noting each time that the word "know" is used. (2) One may lack confidence because he does not understand clearly what assurance means. Usually the problem centers in getting assurance mixed up with emotional feeling. In this case the person should be brought to see that the witness of the Spirit is to the fact of belonging to Christ, whether there is an emotional overflow or not. Romans 8:14–16 would be a good place to see this truth in focus. (3) It is also possible that one does not understand clearly what the conditions are for assurance, in which case attention should be directed to the meaning of repentance and faith as expressed finally in obedience. (4) If the person still does not have the witness, then it could only be due to failure to respond fully to the will of God. Every Christian has the right of knowing that relationship with Christ is a present reality. Biblical evidence for this witness may be found in the Bible study for new Christians entitled *Established by the Word of God* (Huntington Valley, Penna.: Christian Outreach, 1968), or any number of other good follow-up Bible stories.

mitment. The Bible can be used as a reference as needed. If the seeker does not seem to be satisfied, the counselor will need to find out why and to deal with the problem.

When the matter has been resolved, the assured Christian may be invited to bear witness to his faith by offering a prayer of thanksgiving to God. Then friendly counsel may be given regarding basic disciplines of the Christian life.[4] Obedience to all the revealed will of God is the point of particular emphasis. To nail down some of the things that have been said, the person may be left with a Gospel tract or a simple Bible guide for study.[5]

Before the victorious seeker leaves, he should be introduced to others of like mind who will encourage his faith.[6] If someone other than the counselor is to carry on the follow-up, this would be an ideal time to get them together. Such an introduction might also lead to some kind of group association, such as a prayer cell or Bible study fellowship.

---

[4] It is not necessary to go into a long discussion about the necessity of these Christian practices. Usually a few minutes is sufficient at this time. The person simply needs to be reminded to read his Bible every day, with a suggestion as to where he might begin—perhaps a chapter a day in the Gospel of John. Also, he can be asked to remember to pray every day, possibly suggesting a minimum time of fifteen minutes. (Remember he is just a spiritual baby.) Then, of course, he needs to be encouraged to become involved in the church life. The new disciple will readily agree to these things. As time goes on, the follow-up worker can enlarge upon these disciplines in subsequent meetings.

[5] Probably it would be wise to give the person only what he could read within the next day or so. This would mean that the larger Bible study books should be introduced later when there is more leisure to explain their use. Excellent materials may be obtained from the Billy Graham Evangelistic Association, The Navigators, Campus Crusade for Christ, Inter-Varsity Christian Fellowship, Christian Outreach, and other interdenominational organizations. Many denominational publishing houses also offer materials along this line, and of course, a church should use these resources whenever possible.

[6] In making this introduction, give opportunity for the person to express his new commitment. For example, "Bill Smith, would you meet John Doe. I know that he will want to tell you what God has done in his life." This is a very natural way to get the new disciple to share his testimony.

CONTINUING CARE

Hereafter the young disciple should be contacted regularly by a follow-up worker, preferably several times a week. These casual visits need not be long, nor should they appear to be routine. The idea is just to get together as friends and share the things of God.[7]

If it is discovered, through these contacts, that the person still is not clear in his Christian experience, the problem can be resolved now. After all, the person is still seeking reality and he is still open for instruction. It would be nice if everyone had all their fears resolved at first, but it does not work out this way with many people.

Even in the case of those who were genuinely converted, doubtless there will still be hurdles to clear. Where some problem is detected, such as knowing what to do with doubts and temptations, the follow-up worker can deal with it sympathetically out of his own experience and knowledge of the Word. In the same spirit of helpfulness, practical help can be given as questions arise in the realm of personal devotions, family worship, social ethics and witnessing. If the person is doing some kind of prepared Bible study program, the worker can also use these times to good advantage in checking work assignments.

The important thing is to keep the Christian responding to the leading of the Holy Spirit in his life, which will mean minding God in every detail that he understands. Where this is practiced as an inviolable rule of life, every Christian

---

[7] Most of these contacts can be casual meetings in the normal activity of the day—having a coffee break together at work, coming home together on the bus, going out together to a ball game, P.T.A. meeting or church service. The less rigid the visits, the better. However, the informality of these contacts does not minimize the importance of those things which are discussed. Though it may not be immediately apparent to the new Christian, the fellowship friend has a definite purpose in mind in these calls. Progress in the Christian life is expected, and the counselor is always checking up on how things are going. Reports on the progress are then relayed through proper channels to the church officers.

should be full of grace and glory, overflowing with the joy of revival.

All along the way, the Christian life is meant to be victorious, even as it is constantly expanding in the realization of the life of Christ. There will be times of great testing, but through it all the obedient pilgrim should have a shout of victory in his soul, knowing that he walks with the Son of God, whose blood cleanses from all sin, moment by moment. Continuing follow-up consists largely in keeping this truth in focus and interpreting it in life situations as they arise.

GROWTH BY GROUPS

Raising children is a family affair, so more than individual guidance is needed. There needs to be a warm association within the church. Within this company of believers, a Christian learns what it means to be a member of the family of God.

The small group fellowship is the most natural way to provide this environment. As people are brought into the revival, they need to be involved in some kind of close association with others where they can grow together. Already discussed in connection with revival preparation, the group principle applies equally in revival follow-up. In fact, the same pattern that produces revival is the way to keep it.

A confirmation or membership training class may be one way to provide this nurture for the first few months.[8] Where the person-to-person concept of follow-up is in operation, such a class can give helpful structure to a disciplined course

---

[8] The pastor usually is the teacher, though other leaders can handle it. The class normally meets for an hour each week. Basic instruction is given in the doctrine, history and discipline of the church. Normally all persons who come into the fellowship of the church formally are expected to take the course. Manuals for use in these classes can be obtained from any denominational publishing house.

of study. After the course is completed, the group may want to form some kind of continuing fellowship.

CONGREGATIONAL LIFE

Beyond these small groups, every Christian should feel a part of the larger fellowship of the church. Participation in the worship services should become a habit. The same is true of the Sunday school, the missionary society, social functions, retreats—all of these activities help one grow in the family of God and, each in their own way, can contribute to the continuing spirit of revival.

From time to time the Church can have special programs to accentuate spiritual devotion. Some of these services may follow much the same pattern as the revival meeting discussed earlier. The Church does not have to be in a low spiritual ebb to have a spiritual-life crusade. It is much better to have such a series of services when the congregation already enjoys a high degree of Christian experience. Where this is the case, the crusade simply helps to keep the church awake to her responsibilities even as it offers renewed opportunity for an evangelistic harvest.

EDUCATION WITH PURPOSE

All of these means of Christian development should find expression in evangelism. Nurturing the faithful is essential, but as we have seen, it must always be held within the context of the Christian mission to a lost world. Anytime the church becomes preoccupied with her own interests she loses the radiance of the self-giving love of Christ and, unwittingly —in trying to save her life—she loses it.

No temptation is more beguiling than this. After all, is there not a legitimate need to protect the gains of the revival? How then can the revival continue unless its children are nourished in the faith?

Clearly a vigorous educational program is indispensable if the work is to go on. The danger lies in making education of the saints an end in itself. Though it does not have to, the zeal for Christian education has a subtle way of pushing evangelism to the periphery of life. When this happens, not only does the educational program flounder for lack of direction, but the nerve of revival is paralyzed.

The remedy does not lie in minimizing either education or evangelism. Both are essential. One produces soul-winners while the other produces soul-winning. The point is that each must lead to the other. "Education without evangelism makes Pharisees; evangelism without education makes fanatics." [9]

LEADERSHIP THE KEY

The key again is leadership. People are waiting for someone to show them the way. They are generally open to instruction. God has prepared His harvest. The only limitation is harvesters —shepherds who will lead the sheep (Matthew 9:36–38).

The entire program of the church, indeed, the whole course of life, revolves around shepherds. In a very real sense, we are today where our leaders have taken us, and our experience is a reflection of their lives. But, just as we have followed, so also we have led. No person lives unto himself. Whether we live for Christ or self, our witness has its inevitable influence upon those around us who in turn lead others.

The need is for shepherds who themselves are led by the Spirit of Christ—men who follow the Master so consistently that their lives always point the way to Him who is the Great Shepherd of the sheep.

When the church is led by such men of vision and dedication, regardless of the policy followed, there will be continuing fruitfulness. But where this kind of leadership is lacking,

---

[9] George E. Sweazey, op. cit., p. 189. Used by permission.

however excellent the plans and programs may be, the Church will flounder in the slough of aimlessness.

Ultimately, the test of revival is the way in which it reproduces men to lead others. In the final analysis, this is the genius of every enduring spiritual awakening.

As those who have found spiritual strength go forth to show by their changed lives what God has done *in* them, it will not be long before God will show what He can do *through* them. Here is the reward of revival—the satisfaction of seeing the investment of labor returning multiplied dividends in the lives of matured Christians reproducing their kind in an ever enlarging sphere of influence unto the ends of the earth and unto the end of time.

STUDY ASSIGNMENTS
7

PERSONAL STUDY

1. What about young converts makes follow-up imperative? Ephesians 4:14 (I Peter 2:2)

2. How did Paul look upon his relationship to new Christians? I Thessalonians 2:11 (Galatians 4:19)

3. What was there about most of the early church meetings which provided such a good environment for this family relationship? Acts 2:2, 46; 5:42; 12:12; 16:40 (Romans 16:5; I Corinthians 16:19; Colossians 4:15; Philemon 2)

   How can this atmosphere of close informal fellowship be realized in the Church today?

4. What is expected of each person in the family of God according to Ephesians 4:13–15? Sum up your thoughts in a sentence.

5. What about Christ in you especially attests to spiritual development? Ephesians 3:17–19 (I Thessalonians 3:12; I Corinthians 13)

6. What is a normal expression of maturity in terms of practical service? Hebrews 5:12 (I Corinthians 3:1–3)

7. Read Paul's farewell message to the elders of the church at Ephesus in Acts 20:17–38. What does he charge these leaders to remember?

   Why was he so concerned for this great revival church? 20:29, 30

What was the means by which the church was to be built up in the faith according to Acts 20:32?

Yet why do you suppose that Paul gave so much attention to his own example among them for three years? Note 20:17–26; 31, 33–35. In answering this question, think back upon your study of revival all through the Bible, and especially the Gospels.

8. Then if you are to train leaders in the church, what must you do above all else? Philippians 3:17; 4:9 (I Corinthians 11:1)

9. To put this truth in better focus, paraphrase II Timothy 2:2.

10. As you look at your own life, do you see this principle in operation? Are you leading newer Christians in the way of Jesus, and are you teaching them in turn to lead faithful men who will likewise teach others? How? If you are not satisfied, what do you plan to do about it?

Of course, it comes down finally to your own experience of Christ. Do those who look at you see the marks of Jesus? In short, is your life an example of spiritual reality, which is revival?

GROUP DISCUSSION

Since this is your last group exercise in this study it is only natural that you center your concern upon reproduction. The personal Bible study has lifted out the idea, but you need to get down now to the application of these principles in your church. Perhaps it would be well to let each person tell how they were nurtured in the faith during their first Christian years. The home doubtless will be the big stabilizing factor in most instances, as it should be, but what did the church do to help? From here consider the fruitfulness of your present policy. Now would be a good time to lay some plans for definite implementation of any suggestions for improvement.

You may also want to meet again as a group to continue your discussions around the Word of God. It might even be that your group could become a home for others who have found the reality of Christ. Decide together what course you should follow in the future.